Sign This

Sign This

"The Real Truth About Your Sports Heroes and the Sports Autograph Industry"

Tom Bunevich

T&S Publishing

Publisher's Cataloging-in-Publication
(Provided by Quality Books, Inc.)

Bunevich, Tom.
  Sign this : the real truth about your sports
heroes and the sports autograph industry / Tom
Bunevich. -- 1st ed.
    p. cm.
    Includes index.
    ISBN 0-9700227-4-3

    1. Autographs--Economic aspects.   2. Athletes.
3. Sports--Collectibles--Economic aspects.
I. Title.

GV583.B86 2000   796
                                   QBI00-383

Interior Design and Composition by Publishing Professionals, New Port Richey, Florida
Cover Photo by Steve Ribbe
Cover Design by Teresa Thomas
Cover Photo Credits:
Baseball bats—Hillerich and Bradsby Co., Lousiville, KY
Baseball Trading Cards—Pacific Trading Cards, Lynnwood, WA and Playoff Corp., Grand Prairie, TX
Basketball—Spalding Sports Worldwide, Chicopee, MA
Boxing Glove—Everlast Sports, Bronx, NY
Mini-helmets—Riddell, Chicago, IL
Photographs—Photofile, Inc., Yonkers, NY
Sports Illustrated—Time-Warner, New York, NY

Printed in the United States of America

Dedication

This book is dedicated to one special group of people, the best man I've ever known, the best wife on the planet and a supreme being.

First, I want to thank the hundreds of collectors, dealers, and customers that supported my efforts through the years. I can never repay you for your kindness, patronage, and loyalty. Second is my late father, Stan Bunevich, Sr. He will always be my hero and the best man I've ever known. (Read more about him in the conclusion.) Third, to my soul mate and wife Sue. I couldn't have invented a better partner.

You've always allowed me to pursue my dreams. You're always willing to help. Simply put, you are the best. I love you. You've taught me the meaning of love.

Lastly, I dedicate this book to the best decision I have ever made. That was to make Jesus Christ my personal savior in 1979. God has provided me a lifetime of guidance, positive direction and inner peace. I've learned what it is to have a personal relationship with Christ. It's something everyone can have. May God have the glory.

My favorite scripture, Matthew 6:33 reads, "But seek ye first the kingdom of God and his righteousness; and all these things shall be added unto you." God has provided me with all I've ever wanted.

Table of Contents

About the Author

Tom Bunevich graduated from Marshall University in 1975 with a BA in journalism. After obtaining a MA in sports administration in 1982 from Biscayne College (now St. Thomas University) in Miami, Florida, Bunevich entered the sports memorabilia business. He started Bay Area Sports Collectables in Tampa, Florida in 1983.

Tom has worked for a small number of local newspapers, the *Charleston Daily Mail* (WV), *Pittsburgh Post-Gazette* (PA), and Canonsburg (PA) *Daily Notes*. He has written many freelance articles for *Sports Collectors Digest*, *Sweet Spot* and various other publications dealing with the sports collectible industry. From 1991 to 1995, Tom hosted a weekly one hour collectible show on WFNS-Sports radio 910 in Tampa.

After selling his two sports collectible shops in 1989, Tom formed TB Sports Promotions. TB Sports conducted sports collectible shows in Central Florida for eight years, hosting more than 300 sports figure autograph guests for the events. He was a founder and first president of the Florida Baseball Card Dealers Association.

Bunevich is an autograph collector and gained prestige as one of the leading sports collectibles show promoters in the nation. In business from 1983 through 1997, he earned a reputation for honesty, integrity, and quality service. He estimates he has sold more than $2 million worth of autograph signature tickets and items in his 14 years in the industry. Bunevich has worked as Show Manager for *Tampa Tribune* Productions since October 1997. He lives in Tampa with his wife Sue, and sons Matthew and Andrew.

Introduction

Ten minutes after meeting one of my lifelong sports heroes, I wished I hadn't. I had been looking forward to meeting Willie Mays, who had come to Tampa, Florida to be an autograph guest at my card show. It was June 17, 1989 at the Pickett Suite Hotel, and it was quickly turning into a nightmare.

As one who takes pride in his ability to keep things organized, I realized five minutes after Willie started signing some of the 600 items in the room that I had lost control. Willie wasn't using the color pen I had requested, and was carelessly mixing up dealer items so I could no longer identify ownership. Despite my appeals, he refused to cooperate. Finally, three hours later, I gathered all the items, carried them to my automobile, and headed home.

Like a pitcher after a tough loss, on the way home I replayed the previous three hours. Then I thought about the image that I'd had of Mays the night before: a happy-go-lucky, smiling, cooperative gentleman.

Boy, was I wrong.

As one of the leading sports collectible show promoters in the nation from 1983–1997, I saw "up close and personal" the character, attitudes, and behavior of over 300 athletes from various sports, including more than 100 Hall of Famers. I have learned that too many of these sports heroes belie the image we and the media give them. We are too willing to forgive and to overlook their shortcomings and misdeeds. I was guilty of this myself for too long. Now, I want to set the record straight.

I was part of a booming industry that witnessed the sports autograph market rise from the $5 Mickey Mantle autograph to the $500 Bill Russell charged. Once upon a time only the true autograph collector was interested in signatures; now even the novice sports fan is in the game. It all started when signatures became a valuable commodity. As the demand for autographs—especially free ones—grew, access to the athletes tightened and they became less cooperative and concerned. A once-innocent hobby went haywire with price gouging, forgery, cutthroat competition and lack of policing.

This autograph madness took off with the booming sports card and memorabilia business of the late 1980s, when appearances of athletes as guest signers were the rule. Since in most cases I was paying the athletes a stiff fee for their appearance, I was technically their boss for that period. So instead of seeing the athletes as a fan would, awash in all the fame and adulation, I viewed their appearances as business transactions with the intent of selling enough autographs to cover their fees, which can be expensive: I have paid over $81,000 to one former baseball great for an appearance. In conversing with many of these athletes and learning more about them, I've found most live normal day-to-day lives; only their status is elevated in our society because of their athletic achievements.

My time spent with these celebrities has revealed their true characters. I have been able to see what makes some sports heroes good guys and makes others jerks. These encounters over the past 13 years, coupled with feedback from fellow promoters, collectors, and dealers enables me to provide an accurate account of how an athlete's image compares to the real thing.

Told in two parts, the first three chapters of this book are devoted to a study of the sports autograph industry and contains much inside information the general public has never been told. The remainder of the book discusses our sports heroes from my personal perspective. There are many stories to tell.

If you want to know the real truth, sit back and start reading. It'll be a real eye-opener—just like my first encounter with Willie Mays.

As the subtitle suggests, this book will reveal "The Real Truth About Your Sports Heroes and the Sports Autograph Industry." Hopefully, the images you have of your heroes are accurate. If not, I'm sorry the truth hurts.

Finally, I want to thank the hundreds of people who made this book possible—but most importantly, my wife Sue. Her encouragement and love are with me daily.

It's time to get started. There is an incredible amount to tell.

Chapter 1

The Sports Autograph Industry: Blame the 1980s

One afternoon in October 1984, Rick Counts, an agent representing baseball star Dwight Gooden, entered my sports collectibles shop in Tampa to ask whether I would be interested in having an autograph session with Gooden in my store. A fee of $500 didn't seem like much, so we agreed to a two-hour appearance the first Saturday in December.

Gooden was back in Tampa after a stellar rookie season for the New York Mets. His 17-9 pitching record, 2.60 ERA, and 276 strikeouts would earn him the National League Rookie of the Year Award. I promoted the signing through posters, a newsletter, and newspaper advertisements. Figuring the increase in business and sale of merchandise would help to offset the fee, I offered one free autograph and a charge of $2 for each additional signature.

Response was overwhelming: Gooden signed over 700 items, even though we limited the extras. Sales inside the shop totaled eight times that of a regular Saturday, and I had to pay him another few dollars to stay another half-hour and finish the

Dwight Gooden signs December 1984, my first guest. What a turnout. —Photo by Tom Bunevich

line. The local media covered the event, giving my store even more publicity. I thought I'd stumbled onto a gold mine, and so it was the course was set for the next 13 years of my life.

In 1984 the sports autograph industry was in its infancy and still piggybacking on the sports collectibles industry, which was then mainly sports cards. Little was known about fees, charges and value, and few people besides promoters cared. Certainly none foresaw the enormous growth that would take place in the next decade, or that the industry would develop into a full-fledged monster growing increasingly out of control.

Before we discuss specifics about the 1980s, we should realize that autograph collecting and admiring star athletes is not new. Societies have always placed their sports heroes on pedestals. Prior to the 80s, most appearances by athletes were done as public relations or fund-raising gestures, but this changed in the mid-80s when a growing dollar value was attached to their signature.

As the decade progressed, autograph appearances by athletes at sports collectible shows and shops became more frequent. It was a chance for the athlete to meet the public, sign autographs, pose for photos, shake hands, and get paid for it. Prestige was added to the event. Attendance at card shops increased due to these appearances, enhancing card sales. Publicity became easier to obtain because of the guests. Most importantly, it gave the public a chance to meet their heroes in a low key, relaxed environment, and if promoted properly, the public came in ever-increasing numbers. The athlete, in turn, saw opportunity knocking. There was big money to be made at such appearances, especially after retirement. What better way to make money than by signing your name, getting compensated for it, and re-living the glory days?

"My phone just kept ringing," said Bob Allen of Milwaukee, Wisconsin's Bob Allen Advertising, which represents over 300 athletes for such appearances, including 32 exclusives. "There was a market, so anybody wanting to be a promoter figured he could make money at it. Successful shows and appearances led to more requests for more appearances."

Fees were an amount the athlete received for a specific time period. In most cases, a written agreement was completed and the sponsor began his promotion. Depending on the fee, the sponsor would either give away the autograph or issue a charge based on the fee he had to pay. Today, because those fees have risen for even the lesser named athletes, it's virtually impossible to give away free autographs.

Today's superstars can command $50,000 or more for an appearance. Since most of today's athletes can earn more through product endorsement contracts, there's little interest in making such appearances.

"Appearance fees have definitely scared off many promoters," said Gary Nagle of Kissimmee, Florida, who has operated shows in central Florida since 1982. "It's a big risk to bring a major guest. It is certainly different than it was 10 years ago."

Thanks to the growth of the sports autograph industry, there are a number of different types of appearance fees. Most common is the straight up, "I'll give you this much time (two hours, for example) for a certain fee—say, $5,000." The sponsor must also pay the athlete's expenses (airfare, lodging, meals, transportation, etc.) during the appearance. An athlete coming from the west to the east coast can easily incur $2,000 or more in additional cost for the sponsor.

In 1984, Mickey Mantle did appearances offering 800 autographs for $5,000. By 1986, his fee had risen to $10,000. In 1991, it was $40,000 for 1,400 autographs. In 1992, it jumped to $50,000 for those same 1,400 signatures. In 1993, Mantle signed an agreement with Upper Deck®, a California sports card and memorabilia company. His fee through Upper Deck®, who now owned his rights, was set at $50,000 for 800 autographs. Additional expenses for Mantle and a guest, who usually assisted in the autograph sessions and kept track of the numbers, included travel fees, driving the cost even higher. Yet the demand continued despite the rising cost.

In 1990, the fee went to $30 per signature, with Mantle doing a few shows in 1992 with a $40 charge per autograph. Once Mickey became the property of Upper Deck®, the usual fee rose to $75 for each autograph. Mantle also had a number of signing restrictions, meaning he would no longer sign selected items such as unauthorized lithographs, bats, replica jerseys, and baseball gloves. (We'll go into more detail later on this practice).

Of course, the key factor in determining what a promoter will charge for an autograph is the fee. If player A is to receive $4,000 for his two hour appearance and will incur an estimated expense account of $500, the promoter has to guarantee player A those figures. The promoter will then figure in his expected autograph demand based on his experiences and promotional effort. If the promoter believes he will sell 450–500 autographs, he'll price them at $9–$12.

For any shortfalls, the promoter makes up the difference. Therefore, you'll usually see the promoter having the guest sign as many extra items as possible if the turnout is below expectations. He can sell these later at a lower cost to offset some of his losses. This is the way many major autograph dealers are able to purchase inventory at a lower cost. In some cases, a promoter who falls below expectations may restructure the deal on the spot, offering the signer less money for less time, especially if he can't pay the athlete otherwise.

To show the difference in today's autograph market from the mid-1980s, one need only look at the base of predicted autograph sales. In the 80s, demand usually called for 800 to 1,000 signatures for an appearance as opposed to half that today. The extra demand was from dealers, mail order items, and a larger unsatisfied audience.

"Just remember the higher the charge, the more resistance you'll meet," Nagle advises. "You can't rely on much dealer or mail order to help any longer. When you go over $25, you'll have a tough time selling more than one-per-person."

Under TB Sports Promotions, my company that conducted sports collectible shows and signings, I suffered significant losses only three times. One was Mike Schmidt, who generated $32,000 of his $40,000 fee. Second was Duke Snider, a $4,000 loser on a $12,000 fee. The third was Rod Carew, who generated only $12,500 of $16,500.

As appearance fees rose throughout the 1980s, promoters answered with large productions. Shows were developed with a group of signers around a certain theme, giving them a common bond. Promoters could then gather more signers under one roof, attract more dealers and greater attendance, and gain more publicity. Major productions revolved around such themes as the 500 Home Run Club, featuring those in baseball who have hit 500 or more career home runs; the 3,000 Hit Club, those in baseball who had

3,000 or more career hits, and the 300 Game Winners among pitchers. Themes were developed as reunions for championship teams, such as the 1969 Mets and 1975–76 Cincinnati Reds. Fans could pay homage to their heroes in group settings, making all of the participants an easier sell. This enabled the small group of athletes in these exclusive clubs to prosper even more.

Realizing their status, athletes like Ted Williams, Hank Aaron, Willie Mays, and Ernie Banks could demand more for appearances. Shows without the presence of any of them in the theme and the show lacked punch, so promoters were forced to pay the higher fees or do without. Fearing an unsuccessful show, the promoter usually decided to pay the fee.

While the procedure of a fee for time was the standard practice, other methods of appearance payments also rose in the 1980s. Most popular of these alternatives was the "pay per piece" method. An athlete would be paid an amount for every signature. Complicating matters was the fact that counts were often difficult in this high speed situation, and fees varied for signatures on a variety of items.

Though most of the appearances were public autograph sessions, private signings were the first choice for many. These were usually arranged for dealers and mail order customers. The athlete was put into a room with all the items to be signed, and paid upon completion of the signing. This was less hectic, quicker for the signer, and required less preparation and promotion. Smart promoters lined up athletes for such signings when they might already have reason to be in that location for sports or charitable events, thus eliminating travel expenses. Many major order houses often scheduled such appearances when the athlete was in town to play their local team. For example, appearances might be arranged for George Brett in New York when the Royals were in town to play the Yankees.

As the industry grew in the 1980s, so did the need for more information; specialized businesses sprung up to deal with this growth. More promoters, full-time autograph-only dealers, publications, mail order houses, verifying and authenticating services, and corporate partnerships with athletes became prevalent.

The annual national sports collectors' show grew from 500 dealer tables and 15–20 signers in the mid-80s to 900 tables and

40–50 autograph guests by 1994. As the autographs grew to become a higher percentage of the total sports collectibles market, so did the number of dealers and products dealing directly with autographs.

Many full-time autograph dealers went further into the market by specializing in tougher-to-obtain signatures. Deceased Hall of Famers, team baseballs (especially of outstanding or championship teams) and reluctant signers were sought out. High demand for these limited supply items caused a rapid escalation in value. Although demand was greater for current and living Hall of Famers, the competition seemed to focus on current superstars, mainly due to the greater expertise necessary to buy, sell and trade older items. Michael Jordan, Ken Griffey Jr., Emmitt Smith and Dan Marino were easier to sell than the old-timers.

Sellers and buyers wanted to be sure of their products, so authenticating services were established by autograph experts to verify signatures, especially for the older deceased athletes. The "Information Age" had hit sports autographs. Publications such as *Autograph Collector*, *Sweet Spot*, *Tuff Stuff*, *Autograph Times*, and *Sports Collectors Digest* offered price guides, dealer advertising, and stories dealing with the hobby and the characters in it.

Scoreboard, a New Jersey company that entered the big time in the mid-1980s, held private signings with players and started to mass market the items. Using Scoreboard's leadership, the Home Shopping Network began to produce programming with athletes selling their wares and other sports collectibles. This practice continues today.

With Scoreboard, the Home Shopping Network, Upper Deck®, mail order houses, shows, and more shops opening across the country, the market was blanketing the masses, including areas not covered by appearances. Sports autograph sales began to reach the mailboxes and living rooms of America.

But with that growth came growing pains. As fees rose, so did buyer resistance. The days of selling 800–1,000 autographs per session were over by 1992–93, except for rare occasions. The threat of forgeries frightened off many buyers. The media began to question high autograph charges. Promoters stung by losses and appearance fees, smaller crowds and less demand explored other avenues, such as less expensive guests or local athletes that would do the sessions for smaller fees or charitable contributions. Competition at shows turned into a cutthroat war as dealers began selling the same items, and prices dropped as the market became glutted.

Baseball athletes were kings of the signing circuit until the late 1980s, accounting for an estimated 80 percent of the signings until the 1990s. After 1990, football players became increasingly more frequent signers due to generally lower fees, increasing demand, and the opportunity to be new to a geographical area, where, unlike their baseball counterparts, the first appearance drastically reduced the demand.

"Bringing football players to shows was a natural progression," said Allen. "They were still heroes, available, and had reasonable fees. When word got out that they, too, could draw fans, they were offered more appearances. Some draw better than baseball players, although that's mostly a regional issue."

As more athletes hit the autograph circuit, the question of what they should charge for an appearance arose. There was no known formula for an autograph appearance, and in actuality is an individual decision made by the athlete.

Although largely the result of supply and demand, the true value of an autograph includes many other factors, the largest being appearance fees and the promoter's charge. The value of autographs for deceased athletes depends on name recognition and availability. The longer the athlete has been deceased, the more difficult it is to find his signature. Babe Ruth signatures are more difficult to find than any current player, but the high price, authenticating process, and uncertainty of authenticity eliminate many buyers, especially the novice.

Other ingredients that determine value include the athlete's accessibility. For example, it is easier to find a Bob Feller autograph than a Bill Russell signature. Feller has made more appearances than any athlete in the past 15 years and is regarded as a cordial signer; Russell has refused to sign any autographs, except on rare occasions.

Death creates more demand for the autograph and an increase in value. For example, when Don Drysdale died suddenly from a heart attack in 1993, demand was greater than the existing supply and the price rose rapidly from a fee of $25 for a single baseball to $60–$75. Sports collectibles and autograph collector publications ran periodic guides for autographs based on the above factors; in general, the values held true.

After the baseball players' strike of 1994, it was apparent that the public's attitude toward their sports heroes had turned negative. Attendance at shows and signings decreased, creating more financial decisions for the promoters. The number of dealers lessened, although the market was still crowded. The industry had become a victim of simple economics: supply was greater than the demand. A glut existed in supply, and except in rare cases, only older, tough-to-find items in high demand retained value. Inability to police, enforce, and regulate the marketplace, along with constant media focus on possible forgeries also presented major problems for buyers and sellers.

Across the country in 1990, there were an estimated 50–75 shows with major guests. In 1995, the number dropped to 20–25. Many buyers were priced out of the market: there were just too many autographs and items to collect. Promoters looked for cheaper alternatives, such as lesser known or local heroes. Serious collectors stayed with their hobby but became more selective; the casual collector cut back or did without. An industry that had prospered in the 1980s and early 1990s had run its course. The "good old days" of less than 10 years ago were gone forever.

Unfortunately, so were the days of $500 Dwight Gooden appearances. That same appearance today would cost $12,000–$15,000—a risk few promoters are willing to take.

Chapter 2

The Art of Autograph Collecting

Pretend for a moment you are Michael Jordan, the world's most famous athlete. You can't go anywhere without being recognized. Everywhere you go, people want a piece of your time either for an autograph, a photo, or a handshake. You attract an instant crowd . . . and once you begin signing, you can be there for hours.

You have two options: first is to comply by signing autographs and posing for photographs. Your second option is to refuse, which tarnishes your image—especially if your fan is some adoring youngster who has waited for two hours in the hotel lobby.

After a season of being the hunted in NBA cities, you learn to make adjustments. You exit by side doors, stay in different hotels under other names, politely refuse to stop and sign, carry items so your arms are full and you can't stop, find places where you can eat in private, and make arrangements for privacy when making public appearances. Like anyone else, you have bad days where you don't want to be bothered.

Meanwhile, you see the autographs you sign being sold in the marketplace—$100 for the basketball you signed, $75 for the photo. You become more disturbed when one collector hands you five photos to sign; although you certainly don't need the money, signing things to see them sold bothers you. However, there's little you can do.

If you are Michael Jordan, you just go on, realizing this is the price of success. But if you're the autograph collector, you've either been able to get Jordan's autograph or not. You might have made five trips to the hotel and come up empty, or succeeded in the first ten minutes. It's almost like hunting; success can come quickly, or never.

There are do's and don'ts that rule the autograph market. Collecting sports autographs depends on one's desire, available time, location, cash flow, opportunity, and perseverance. Whether a novice or serious collector, one must take advantage when an opportunity presents itself. Preparation and knowing the shortcuts can improve success.

There are many reasons that collectors pursue their passion or hobby, but it was the dollar value added to the item that began the collector boom starting in the 1980s. The signatures on baseballs, footballs, photographs, books, and memorabilia gave collectors not only a piece of their heroes, but a marketable, tangible commodity.

"I doubt many people would collect if there wasn't money involved," said Rodney Archibald of Tampa, an autograph collector since 1985. "I've seen more interest in what it's worth than the fact that they got the player's autograph. I collect because I enjoy the chance of meeting the athlete or celebrity and seeing what he or she is like in person. I get something I can keep for life, knowing that the person actually signed it."

If one is going to pursue autographs, he should first know the language. Terminology is important for mail order or show customers. Often, it's taken for granted that those who read the advertisements or attend shows understand the terminology. Here is a glossary of terms for autograph collectors:

1. Amateur night—serious autograph collector's term for novices trying to obtain autographs, usually when they are free.

2. Authenticate—to prove the genuineness and truth of the article/signature. A certificate of authenticity is a document given to provide proof.

3. Auto pen—mechanical device used to trace an autograph, resulting in one that looks like the original but was never signed by that person; usually done to answer mail.

4. Commemorative—piece done to remember, recall a historic date, event, or person, usually limited in number.

5. Dealer—one who sells, buys, and trades in autographed items.

6. Equipment—items worn or used by players, such as hats, bats, uniforms, helmets, gloves, etc. Game-used equipment has actually been used in an athletic contest by a team or a player. Examples include home or road uniforms or jerseys.

7. Fine-point—type of writing pen or Sharpie®, blue pen on baseballs or paper items; fine point blue Sharpie® on photographs, bats, magazine covers.

8. First-day cover—special envelope commemorating the first day of an event, usually indicated with postage mark of date and place.

9. Flat—term for any item to sign that lays flat, such as a sports card, photo, or magazine.

10. Forgery—an autograph sold as truly signed by the athlete, but which was not and passed on as authentic.

11. Fountain pen—old writing pen worked by dipping in an ink well, then transferring onto object; autographs of many deceased early sports heroes are available only in this fashion.

12. "Hound"—slang term for one who chases free autographs, at locations such as hotels, charity events, athletic facilities, or whatever opportunity exists; they "hound" players into signing.

13. HOF/ROY/MVP/CY—short for Hall of Fame, Rookie of the Year, Most Valuable Player, and Cy Young awards; usually followed with a number indicating the year; they serve as time-savers for signers.

14. Goal Line Art—series of postcards done to honor pro football Hall of Famers and great moments in football history.

15. Lithograph—a reproduced painting or drawing, usually limited in number; most athletes refuse to sign unapproved ones.

16. Memorabilia—collective term for all items, used as remembrance of a person, place, event, or combination of these.

17. Mint Condition—top quality condition, usually indicating close to its original state as possible.

18. Panel—part of a baseball not near lettering or the sweet spot.

19. Perez-Steele—series of postcards done to honor baseball Hall of Famers and great moments in baseball history.

20. Personalize—to add more to a signature, such as a name (To Tom:), greeting, statistics, etc. As a general rule, names generally make autographs worth less, statistics worth more.

21. Premier item—used to refer to a signed item that once autographed, brings an even greater increase in value, such as balls, jerseys, helmets, bats, and equipment.

22. Private signing—autograph session not open to the public.

23. Postpaid—postage fee included in price.

24. Publication—collective term for items in printed mode, including magazines, programs, yearbooks, price guides, and any other printed sports matter.

25. Replica—an accurate copy of an item, but not the real thing.

26. Rubber stamping—process by which an autograph is duplicated with rubber stamp and pad, done by many to answer mail.

27. Sharpie®—Sanford writing instrument similar to thin magic marker, used to sign most publications, photos, and bats. Preference is for blue, fine point.

28. Single-signed—item is signed by one person only; opposite is multi-signed, or autographed by many.

29.   Sweet spot—the backside of a baseball opposite the lettering, on official league ball between Rawlings and Cushioned Cork Center; preferred spot for single-signed baseballs.

30.   Throwback—replica piece of equipment of former uniform, helmet, jersey of a particular team.

Whether a "hound," dealer, serious, or novice collector, there are three ways to obtain autographs. Each has its advantages and disadvantages, depending on available time and funds. The three methods are in person, by mail, or by direct purchase.

In person, one can obtain autographs at show appearances, hotels, athletic facilities, public functions, charity events, or even at the athlete's residence. Easiest is the show appearance as you simply buy a ticket, wait your turn, and have your item signed. At the hotel, athletic facility, or public function, success will be determined by the size of the crowd seeking the autographs, the hotel policy (more hotels are prohibiting autograph seekers), your access and the attitude of the athletes, timing and other factors like being prepared and knowing your subjects.

Timing is most important. Be prepared to spend long hours in lobbies, corridors, outside restaurants, and in front of buildings. Players can take side entrances and jump into an already waiting vehicle. I once waited five hours in the hotel lobby looking for Joe Montana, only to be told he'd left through a side door two hours earlier.

Refusals to sign are becoming more common. Some teams have reputations for players reluctant to sign at any time. These teams often have more winning success and star players; common sense dictates they have more demand. Crowds are smaller for teams with less winning traditions and fewer established stars. Some players limit themselves to signing particular items, while others refuse to sign items depicting them with former teams—especially those they left with unpleasant memories. Other times athletes will not sign items that will drastically increase the item's value, such as baseball bats, lithographs, or materials not licensed by professional leagues or player associations.

"Refusals or signing restrictions are becoming more common," says Greg Kempton, a Tampa collector and part-time dealer.

"Guys will say, 'Catch you later,' when they have no intention of coming back. At a show you have to pay for it, but at least you're assured you'll get the autograph and it's real."

In many cases, the athlete will leave the elevator and walk briskly through the front lobby to a waiting bus or cab. The approach is important if the early bird is to get the worm. Most collectors have a system for quick location of a particular item, such as arranging items like sports cards to be signed in alphabetical order. Often, a collector has to walk alongside the athlete as he signs, realizing that is the only way to obtain the signature. It is also important to check that you have the right color pen and that it does indeed write, especially in a crowded situation.

At a charity function such as a banquet or golf tournament, athletes are generally more cordial and cooperative, but they should be approached before the event. In all cases, approaching the potential signer in a polite manner increases the chances of obtaining the signature.

Two key points must be made about the "hound." First, he must not be shy and must be persistent, but not pushy. He must approach his subject, as an athlete won't stop without being asked. Second, he must stay alert; his opportunity may be a ten-second walk from the elevator to a waiting ride. Being in the right place at the right time, learning your layout, exits, the signing habits of your subjects, and having your items ready increases your chance of obtaining an autograph.

Using the mail can produce success in securing autographs, but presents a dilemma regarding verification. Besides rubber stamping and auto pens, athletes have been known to have relatives, clubhouse attendants, and others sign their name and return the items. There are reports that Joe DiMaggio's sister signed much of his mail in his playing days and that the two signatures are difficult to tell apart. In all mail requests, a polite letter and self-addressed stamped envelope increase the chances of return.

More reliable than direct mail to a player's home is to send your item to show promoters or in care of private signings. Publications such as *Sports Collectors Digest, Tuff Stuff, The Autograph Collector*, and *The Beckett Baseball Card Monthly* price guide contain advertisements for shows and private appearances featuring opportunities to obtain autographs through the mail. Authenticity is easy because an autograph ticket stub or certificate of authenticity is usually returned with the signed item. Smart promoters and mail order houses provide a seal or sticker to verify the signature.

When I accepted mail order items, I always handled them with extreme care. I attempted to have them signed as requested, although sometimes the requests were risqué, offbeat, or unusual. I would then send the item back as fast as possible, along with a ticket stub.

If you use this method, make sure you put your name on the items, even if it is in pencil. Be specific with your instructions (color, place, special wording, etc.). Use Post-it® Notes on the item. Make sure you include funds for return postage and insure the item, if desired.

Archibald, who sends items to both the mailing addresses of the athletes and to promoters with the athletes doing show appearances, says the mail has provided him with many signatures he couldn't have gotten otherwise. "Since many athletes don't return regular mail, the only access you might have is a show or private appearance," he reports. "Generally, you'll get a better quality signature by paying for it. Some athletes return mail, but it may take as long as a year—by then you've forgotten about it."

According to Bob Pressley of Marietta, Georgia's B.P. Sports Enterprises who promotes shows, private appearances and has a full-time autograph shop, athletes prefer the private route. "An athlete can sit down, sign uninterrupted and not have to stop for photos, handshakes, and conversation," says Pressley, who has promoted such signings and shows since 1986. "They also like the fact most private appearances are paid in cash. With shows, there's usually more accounting."

The third method of collecting autographs is to just buy them outright. This is the most dangerous way of buying a potential fake, since forgery is a constant problem. Since the buyer is simply placing his trust in the seller and dealer reputation plays a major role, a buyer may never know he was sold a fake.

"Forgery became a big problem because as the industry grew, there was no way to nip it in the bud," said Frank Schnorrbusch of Frank's Sports Center in St. Petersburg, Florida. A dealer for 18 years, Schnorrbusch says that as forgery became more rampant, there was little way to fight back. "It wasn't a high priority among police because of the time involved to prove the case," said Schnorrbusch. "Sometimes the forgery is so good you can't tell the real thing from the fake. There is no national industry, governing body, or promoter group to screen dealers. Getting to the source is almost impossible."

My tip is to forget the handwritten certificate of authenticity or the story about how Aunt Mary got the autograph. Insist on a ticket stub from a private signing or show appearance, or a stamped seal or sticker from the source. Always get a lifetime, money-back guarantee and the name, address, and phone number of the dealer. Price should never be as important as peace of mind.

After you've obtained the item, protect it: buy protective holders and cases and keep it away from sunlight and fluorescent lighting and humidity—the enemies of pens and Sharpies®.

Concerning forgeries, common sense would suggest that most occur in older, harder to find autographs. Surprisingly, the opposite is true for a number of reasons. The main reason is that it is hard to duplicate items of a previous era, such as official baseballs, footballs, and publications. Usually the items will show aging: fading of the signatures, yellowing, fragile pages, and various degrees of wear.

Another reason is that those who collect older autographs are more knowledgeable about their subjects. Dealers often spend more time verifying the authenticity of an older autograph. Also, most older items—before the 1960s—are multi-signed. Since there were fewer autograph collectors in those days, signatures were looked upon more as keepsakes than investments.

Additionally, demand for the current player and living Hall of Famer exceeds that of the older long-deceased athlete. Among today's most sought-after autographs are those of Ken Griffey Jr., Michael Jordan, Tiger Woods, Mickey Mantle, Ted Williams, Brett Favre, Cal Ripken, Frank Thomas, and Joe Montana.

Ironically, these are also some of the most forged autographs in the business. Except for Mantle, who died in 1995, these athletes either make few or no personal appearances. Supply never seems to meet demand, which keeps the values high. This also invites forgery.

"It's fashionable for those doing forgeries to concentrate on guys that are a fast sell," Pressley reports. "The demand is steady enough that they can be brought into the marketplace with little question, then sold for a fast turnaround. It also helps that their signatures are consistent with little change. Once it's perfected, it's an easy sell."

"Prosecution is a major problem," adds mail order dealer Richard Moody of Moody's Sports Autographs in Warner-Robbins, Georgia. "It's tough to prove the case. Law enforcement officials have to ask whether it's worth their time and effort to pursue the case. The final judgment ends up being a slap on the wrist. It's a shame we've even got to talk about this."

Regional heroes make for high demand in their local markets. Atlanta Braves autographs sell extremely well in Georgia, while players like NFL Hall of Famer Lee Roy Selmon may have little demand outside the Tampa area, where he played for the Buccaneers from 1976–84.

Players have begun to fight back over unauthorized sales of their autographs and the possible sale of autographs they see as fake. Professional league representatives are spending more time investigating the autograph market, as are law enforcement officials. Player agents often send notices to dealers asking them to discontinue the sale of autographs for their athlete. Eventually, lawsuits will follow.

Sports leagues and player organizations have reacted to the autograph craze with fences, private signings, security personnel, and man-made boundaries, all reducing access to athletes. Fees have reduced athlete appearances, although teams are now seeking to involve more players in appearances for charity.

Tiger Woods began to limit the items he would sign shortly after his first major win in 1997. He said he would no longer sign photos, golf balls, and items he knew had an instant marketability, but he would sign Nike® (one of his sponsors) items and programs. Guards often escorted him to events with the standard line, "Sorry, no autographs." (We'll discuss more on the athletes and their attitudes in the next chapter.)

As more and more "hounds" join the pack, athletes increasingly become the hunted, leading to more confrontations with fans.

Show appearances have allowed fans to meet their heroes in less chaotic conditions, where attitude and actions reveal much about their true character. As I've found, paying the athlete for appearances is no guarantee of a pleasant experience. They can be princes or jerks.

The next chapter will discuss the behavior, attitude, and actions that determine whether they are princes or jerks in the eyes of collectors and fans. Some of their behavior is shocking, and shatters many a carefully created image.

Chapter 3

Has He Always Been a Jerk Like That?

The majority of athletes regard autograph hounds as pests, but most realize they are part of the territory that comes with notoriety. How autograph seekers regard athletes is another thing: it is individual personality that determines how he is viewed. Some athletes are cooperative and pleasant, while others exhibit the most boorish behavior.

Some legends, such as basketball great Bill Russell, will not sign autographs except at a paid session. Brooks Robinson is the opposite, often going out of his way to accommodate autograph seekers. For these two, this is an established pattern. For others, it is the situation that often dictates the behavior of the athlete. Again, being at the right place at the right time is vitally important.

There are various stages through which athletes progress that shape much of their future attitude and behavior. Collegiate athletic accomplishments initially elevate many athletes to celebrity status; for some, as early as high school.

It is advancement into the professional ranks and the degree of success at that level that determines fame. Most young professional athletes develop a cooperative, "glad to sign it" attitude. This seems to indicate the arrival of the athlete to *bona fide* celebrity status. He enjoys the attention.

As that young athlete progresses and demands on his time increase, autograph requests are no longer the thrill they once were. If he achieves stardom, those demands become even greater.

In sports, one play or game can make a household name. Witness the cases of Bobby Thomson, whose home run in 1951 won the pennant for the New York Giants and has been called "the shot heard around the world." Thomson was an average player until that homer, but almost 50 years later he is still remembered for it. At the opposite end is Bill Buckner, first baseman for the 1986 Boston Red Sox, whose error helped the New York Mets defeat the Red Sox. Though he had an above average major league career, his name will be forever associated with the miscue.

Serious autograph collectors also swear that signatures of athletes in the early days of their careers are neater than their later years. As athletes become more established they learn to write quicker, take shortcuts, and write on the run. In many cases, the signatures actually change as the young star progresses up the ladder. Initials, sloppiness, and poor penmanship become more commonplace.

While most athletes realize that autographs are a part of the business, they also become skilled in ways of avoiding signing them. These methods include using side or kitchen entrances, filling hands and arms so they have a reason not to stop, just saying "No," walking fast, using security, or refusing to sign certain items. However, hounds will tell you there are two main reasons/excuses that accompany the majority of refusals: "Not now, I'll catch you later," and "If I sign for you, I'll have to sign for everybody." These are especially good alibis in crowded areas.

"If I had a quarter for every time I've heard, 'I'll catch you later,' I would be a millionaire," says Archibald. "In most cases, it gets the athlete off the hook. Some actually sign later, but the majority have no intention of doing so. It helps them avoid stopping. You know they're lying, but you also know better than to call them on it or you'll never get the autograph."

Athletes can control entire crowds of autograph seekers with their words, behavior, or actions. I once saw former Detroit Tiger outfielder Kirk Gibson address a crowd of hounds outside the Tigers' clubhouse in Lakeland, Florida with this statement: "I'll sign one for each of you—but the first person who asks me twice, I'll be done for everyone." Nobody dared asked for a second signature Gibson took about 15 minutes to sign for an estimated 100 people. Now *that's* how you handle a crowd!

From my years of soliciting autographs, as well as from speaking with many hounds, I have determined that there are five personality types when it comes to athletes signing autographs. The first is the most cooperative type. I call this the "glad I could" type.

Second is the "grin and bear it" type. In this situation the athlete may not be overjoyed with the idea of signing, but he smiles and endures it, realizing it's part of the obligation of celebrity. His cooperation level often depends on the size of the crowd. Generally, this is the athlete that limits autographs to one-per-person.

The third personality type is the "my bark is bigger than my bite" athlete. This one greets autograph seekers with a statement like, "I'm not going to sign—I don't have time." Then he'll stop and sign. When the crowd grows, he'll take off and say, "I gotta go." Often this athlete prefers children and youngsters over adults, and will usually sign as long as things stay orderly.

The fourth type of personality is the "let's get this over with" signer. He will usually sign—but sloppily, and will refuse notations and posing for photographs. He's just doing the bare minimum. This is the most likely candidate for private entrances and quick exits and usually, you've got to get him on the run. He'll never say much; he just signs quickly and moves on to the next request.

The last type is the "limited access" guy. He'll do all he can to avoid the crowd by walking with security guards, teammates in a large group, or using private entrances. Even if you see him, you have to stop him. Occasionally he signs for a larger group, but most of the time you'll need a one-on-one limited access opportunity for him to sign. One almost has to trap him to get a signature.

Autograph seekers also point out the many differences between the retired and current athlete. I call it the "old school" versus the "new breed." Athletes of the pre-1970s and the 1980s seem to fall somewhere in between, but are still motivated more by personal attitudes, their feelings towards the autograph industry, and the size of the crowd.

The "old school" athletes—mostly those who played before 1960—were the first to capitalize on the autograph appearance fee. They found they could supplement their income by making such appearances. Their fees were, and still are, much less expensive.

Members of the "new breed" differ in many ways. They have little trouble saying "no." They aren't fond of appearances, and set high fees to discourage interest. When they do appear, most will fall into the "limited access," "let's get this over with," and the "grin and bear it" types of personalities. They are more attuned to the value of autographs, and thus more aware of what they are signing and its place in the collector world. There's more awareness of resale potential, and less regard for the fan's opinion of the athlete.

In 1995, I hosted 73-year-old baseball Hall of Famer George Kell at an autograph signing in Tampa. Kell took his time on each ball, writing slowly and deliberately to give everyone a neat, uniform signature. I asked him why he wasn't going faster, as I was worried about completing the necessary number in the prescribed three hours.

"I want everyone that came to get my best," Kell said. "That means taking my time and doing it right. I'll stay as long as I have to. I just want it right. That's the least I can do—after all, they're the ones who paid for the signature and waited in line for it."

One portion of the "old school" involves black athletes of the 1950s. These athletes often carry a chip on their shoulders, directly attributable to the treatment they received while integrating professional sports.

All the promoters I interviewed agreed with my assessment that the majority of black players from the 1950s and early 60s have developed a callous attitude toward autograph seekers. Greats such as Hank Aaron, Willie Mays, Frank Robinson, Bill Russell, Willie McCovey, and Bob Gibson have little trouble refusing requests. My theory is that this hardened attitude may be due to the years of racial taunts and torment.

"It's there, no doubt," said NFL Hall of Famer Lenny Moore, who discussed the topic with me while in a 1996 appearance. "We all went through it. It's tough to let go, but you have to. Some guys haven't. But you still have to understand there were some very trying and difficult times."

While athletes often come under criticism by autograph seekers, many times it is the autograph seeker who is at fault. Hounds sometimes want multiple signatures, items signed with specific notations, send children or bystanders for additional autographs, and generally make pests of themselves.

Many athletes develop personal policies in dealing with hounds. These include signing only specific items, one-per-person, personalization only (to a particular person), no hotel or game day autographs, or children only. Once they're wise to the policy, hounds can adjust. I once saw one pay the busboys and kitchen personnel to obtain autographs of Joe DiMaggio after Joe had placed a one-per-person limit. The $6 baseball attained a value of $75 with Joe's autograph on it, so the $5 paid to the busboys was a wise investment for the hound.

Writing on glossy photographs and bats can be erased with rubbing alcohol or a product called GOOFOFF®, sold in most hardware stores. Ink erasers can take signatures off baseballs. Smart hounds will first preview the quality of the signature by having an index card done first before placing an item of value before the athlete.

The degree of conversation between the hounds and the athlete will vary, depending on their respective personalities. In most cases little is said and the item is simply signed and returned. A smart strategy is to converse with the athlete about a pleasant memory in his past. In the paid appearance setting, most of the conversation between athlete and autograph seeker involves a specific time and achievement, such as the 1958 World Series "when you got that big hit."

"Most of the time, the conversation depends on the size of the autograph crowd," says Archibald. "When it's a bigger crowd the celebrity just wants to get done. You're more likely to have a conversation when there's a smaller crowd."

Based on my 13 years of experience, I have developed a list of 25 ways in which the athlete can offend and thus be classified as "jerks" by autograph seekers. Word spreads fast among hounds, promoters, and collectors about these reputations. The 25 are:

1. Refusing to sign no matter what the circumstances, with lame excuses such as promising to do it later, saying he doesn't have the time, or just ignoring the request.

2. Refusing to cooperate during the signing by ignoring conversation, special requests, disallowing photographs,

and carrying on private conversations while signing requests.

3. Using the wrong color when a specific one is requested or has already been used on a multi-signed item.

4. Scribbling: poor penmanship, especially in the later stages of a sessions.

5. Shortcuts: writing "D Stry" instead of "Darryl Strawberry."

6. Writing upside down on an item, especially if it has been previously signed correctly.

7. Being uncooperative with fans who have paid for an autograph for refusing a simple request like a handshake, photograph, question, or quick notation on an item.

8. Writing in the wrong place when it has been specifically requested and noted.

9. Writing over the names or faces, and in hard-to-see dark areas.

10. Forcing fans to beg for signatures.

11. Cheating on expenses, such as cashing in airline tickets for lower fares, or excessive hotel/food expenditures.

12. Charging extra for items at the show, including changing fees for specific items, even though it wasn't previously mentioned.

13. Being late, especially without a justifiable reason.

14. Mind not on the work: just going through the motions.

15. Purposely going slowly in order to be paid extra to finish.

16. Refusing to sign mail or dealer items, even though it was part of the agreement.

17. Putting the wrong information on the item, such as an improper year or number.

18. No personalization: this limits those who truly collect for enjoyment and not so much for investment. (It's a belief of mine that many athletes do not want to be forced to spell anything especially names.)

19. Smudging or smearing items, especially when it is a multi-signed item, thereby ruining other signatures and lessening the overall value.

20. Bad-mouthing others and generally just being negative.

21. Complaining about the fee, number of autographs, rate, long line, number of items a specific person has, or time left.

22. Limitations: many times a person wants a specific item that the athlete won't sign.

23. Refusing media contact, despite the fact it could create more publicity about the appearance.

24. Making promises to kids such as sending a jersey or hat, when there is no intention on fulfilling the promise.

25. Displaying disapproval of specific requests with an attitude that says, "I really don't want to do this, but I will."

The brief moment in time in which one gets to meet the athlete can be a lifelong memory—but that memory is not always positive. One collector told me that as a youth she worshiped Eddie Mathews. But after seeing him at a show smoking and drinking whiskey during the day while signing autographs, she could only shrug her shoulders.

"You want to believe your heroes will be young forever," she said sadly. "You also want to believe they have godlike qualities. Seeing Eddie after the years of hard living made me realize nobody's perfect. It's still tough to take."

Now that I've provided an overview about the autograph industry and the characters in it, it's time to tell you more about the athletes we've grown to love and hate.

We've seen much of them as players, but what about their behavior off the field? You're about to meet the jerks, good guys, and "just average Joes" of sports, and to learn how they are regarded in the autograph industry by those who work within it.

Chapter 4

My Top Ten Jerks

Based on personal experiences, interviews with promoters and autograph collectors and hounds, here are my Top Ten Jerks:

1.   Willie Mays

2.   Rickey Henderson

3.   Errict Rhett

4.   Mike Schmidt

5.   Darryl Strawberry

6.   Reggie Jackson

7.   Joe DiMaggio

8.   Pete Rose

9.   Gaylord Perry

10.   Denny McLain

Willie Mays

Willie Mays qualifies for the top spot because the behavior I spoke of in my introduction is commonplace with this former Giant great. Forget a free autograph from Mays, as he rarely grants them.

During signing sessions, Mays has been known to walk out when in his estimation the situation becomes chaotic and unruly. You can forget about Mays looking up for photographs or posing for them; he won't do it. If you're counting the autographs, his number is gospel—whether it's right or wrong.

Willie Mays, with the family. Getting a smile from Willie is a rarity.—Photo by Joanne Thresher

I believe Mays truly doesn't care what the public thinks of him. He's not afraid to voice his displeasure with the media, as he usually refuses interviews. I've hosted him four times in public autograph sessions, and he is indeed a huge draw. It's evident the public regards him as a icon, and remembers him by film clips of the smiling, bow-legged youngster dashing around the bases or after the ball. Instead, what they get is a quick signature, little if any exchange, and a view of the top of Mays' head.

Over the years, the influence of two people has created periods of better behavior. The first was Leo Durocher, Mays' first and favorite manager; the second was Carl Keisler, his longtime financial advisor.

The first time I hosted Mays was in 1989. The fourth time was in 1995. By then, Willie had mellowed some and was more cooperative, but still generally unresponsive to the public. At the first meeting, I had to almost beg for personalizations and inscriptions; at his latter appearances, I paid extra for them.

What's troubling about Mays is that he truly is an American hero. In a time when he should be basking in the glory of one of the greatest careers in baseball history, he seems a bitter, mean man who never learned to enjoy adulation and fame. I don't know the reasons for his behavior and attitude, but I, along with thousands who have seen these actions, clearly dislike the Mays they have produced.

In short, if you worship the ground Willie Mays walks on, do yourself a favor and stay away when he's making an appearance. You'll get an autograph, but not much more.

Rickey Henderson

If ever a player gave me a lesson in economics, it was Rickey Henderson. I paid much more money than originally agreed because of the attitude and behavior I got from the career stolen base leader.

Rickey knows how to turn on the charm, especially for youngsters and adoring females. He was cooperative and courteous to the public. At the time I hosted him in 1990, he was at the height of his popularity and drew a huge crowd. When you see Rickey in public it's a 50–50 bet whether he'll sign. Much depends on the size of the crowd, which he will avoid if possible.

My beef with Rickey is that he's been known to play games in signing sessions that enables him to pocket additional dollars at the promoter's expense. First, it's my belief that Henderson and his representative, Aaron Turner, flew in from the Bahamas at a much cheaper cost than the San Francisco flights I had paid for. They had done a show in Miami the week before mine, and it's my guess that they pocketed the difference.

Also, in contract negotiations Turner assured me that I would be able to get 1,000 autographs in the contract's three-hour signing period. I feel Rickey deliberately slowed his pace in the last hour in order for me to have to pay him extra for the 50 autographs (at $18 each) left over after the deadline.

Also, at the private signing the night before the public session, Rickey changed the fee to autograph a bat from $15 to $20, although the contract made no such stipulation. With 120 dealer bats, I felt forced to pay the extra $2, even though I had collected only $18 from dealers. I didn't want to risk an uncooperative Henderson the next day.

Henderson did make one statement that a few of my friends often repeat to this day. When he informed me that he wouldn't sign the 120 bats for $15 each, he looked me in the eye and said, "I can't sign bat-sizz that cheap." I wanted to laugh, but money was at stake. We learned the plural of "bat" that night although we'd always thought it was "bats."

Rickey can be a charmer. He left a positive impression with the public, but not with this promoter. A year later, Turner called me and asked me if I would be interested in bringing Rickey back for an appearance. I politely declined. Apparently other promoters have heard too, because Henderson does few appearances nowadays.

Errict Rhett

The only agent I've ever written to complaining about an athlete's behavior was Errict Rhett. I hosted Errict after he was the National Football Conference's Offensive Rookie of the Year following the 1994 season. Being a former Florida Gator to go along with his Tampa Bay Buccaneer hero status, he was a large draw.

He was contracted to sign for me for two hours, then in private for dealers for another hour. The first hour Errict was all business. But midway through the second hour, things changed. First it was a bathroom break, then a ten-minute private phone conversation while on my clock, slowing the pace to a crawl, and finally meeting with friends while signing the items.

I had received about 80 items in the mail to be signed. As it became apparent that there wouldn't be time for these, Errict told me I would have to pay him for extra time.

I paid him an extra $500 to finish the last 50 items, then delivered him to the private signing area. I left to go to the airport to greet my next day's guest, Kareem Abdul-Jabbar. Upon returning about two hours later, both dealers who had contracted for the hour informed me they also had to pay Rhett $500 more to have their items signed, complained that he wanted more for autographs on premier items and would only sign a limited number of each. Errict left in a haste—with many complaints from these dealers about his actions, demands and behavior.

I wrote Rhett's agent two days later, explaining I thought he had taken advantage of all three of us. I was told there would be no further discussion from Rhett. Once word got out of this ordeal, Errict would not be offered any additional appearances in Tampa.

Of course, Rhett would later overplay his hand and participate in a half-season holdout. The public and team turned on him. He would later be demoted to second team, never to regain a starting spot. In 1998, he left the Buccaneers as a free agent.

Errict Rhett was a classic case of letting success go to one's head.

Mike Schmidt

As mentioned previously, Schmidt holds the distinction of being the largest money loser I've ever had. It was his attitude and behavior during his signing session that turned me off this all-time home run king for a third baseman.

Despite the high charge for the time period of $40 and $50, Mike thought it was a speed contest and went sailing through the items. People didn't even have a chance to ask him a question. He held the pen and Sharpie® in the same hand and quickly moved from one item to the other. For that price, people expected Mike to at least look up. His attitude indicated he just wanted to get things over with and get out of there. I've seen Mike at golf tournaments and public functions and he generally allows one autograph per person, which is certainly fair. However, given the first chance to avoid the crowd or skip out, he'll jump on it.

Frankly, I didn't get a much of a chance to speak with Mike. He was in and out. Feedback from those who paid for the autograph clearly indicated dissatisfaction with the lack of interaction and conversation. Schmidt needs to slow down and smell the roses. Sure, he was booed big time in Philadelphia—but he still has the credentials to be a hero to many. My advice is to enjoy it.

Darryl Strawberry

Given Darryl Strawberry's well documented troubles with spousal abuse, drug rumors, and tax evasion, it would be easy to kick him when he's down. However, after hosting Strawberry in

1989 at the height of his popularity with the Mets, I came away with a less than positive opinion of the former number one draft pick.

First, let me say Strawberry was a great draw. He signed almost 1,200 autographs at $10 each, which at that time was considered a high charge for any athlete. I found him to be somewhat programmed with the standard answers. It was obvious that the Mets were coaching him to say all the right things in their media training sessions.

The night before his appearance, I hosted him in his hotel room for a short private signing. Since Strawberry was the hero for ten-year-old David Kors, son of close friend Terry Kors, Sr. of Tampa, I let David tag along. In Darryl's conversation with David, I remember Strawberry telling David he would send him a bat or jersey. It would never happen. After a year, David finally gave up. Not wanting to let his son down, Terry explained that David's hero probably forgot, or lost his name and address. Terry confided in me he didn't think he'd ever see anything from Strawberry.

During the signing, the quality of Strawberry's signature got worse as he signed, the last half of them nothing more than a "D" and an "S" each followed by a few scribbles. Even Strawberry became "Stby." The public complained, but I could say little. Granted, it was a long name, but with no time limit for the signing and the public paying for the autograph, you'd think Darryl could have done better.

Strawberry also had little trouble saying "no" in public situations and learned to walk quickly and sign. To his defense, he was one of the star Met players in a time when they were a quality and popular team. Crowds followed them.

Darryl went high to the top of the mountain, only to fall to the bottom. To his credit, he worked his way back to the big leagues. Then he was arrested for solicitation in Tampa. Perhaps the demand for a left-hander power hitter outweighs how many chances one should get. He's out again because of a probation violation.

One thing that impressed me about Strawberry was his tall, muscular build. It was obvious he had the physical gifts; the question was his mental approach. When I hosted him, he was a brash, cocky youngster who came off as a real jerk.

Reggie Jackson

Reggie Jackson is the most arrogant athlete I've ever met. He can be polite to one person and nasty to the next. His sense of humor can be funny or biting. He'll usually refuse autograph requests and can be two different people under these circumstances. It's the presence of a cameraman or newspaper photographer that makes "Mr. October" turn into "Mr. Cooperative." Take away the lenses and you'll most likely see "Mr. Nasty."

In my session with Reggie I saw both sides. When a paying customer asked for "Mr. October" with his autograph, Reggie might consent to one and flatly refuse another fan with the same request. Reggie doesn't hide his emotions well and it's obvious when he disapproves—he tells you.

One thing Reggie taught me was that open expense accounts can be deadly. I had agreed to pay for two nights of lodging in separate rooms as well as one day of meals for Reggie and his representative. In addition, I had to pay for a first class and regular airfare from California to Tampa, totaling almost $2,000.

Since I had left my credit card at the hotel (a common practice in these situations), all charges were placed on that card. Upon check-out before the signing, the bill came to over $750. I had expected about $400 since the rooms were $75 per night. I figured the maximum they could eat was $100 total in a day.

When the bill was handed to me at the show, I was stunned. What also bothered me was that Reggie and his partner simply dusted off the total, saying, "We'll just sign more items." Already needing about 750 autographs to break even and struggling to get there, this was not what I wanted to hear. But rather than ruin the signing session for those paying for the signature, I decided to drop the issue until later. When I brought the issue up again, I was met with the same response. Realizing I had better take what I could get, Reggie signed a few more items and said we'd call it even. I never got an explanation or an apology.

Examining the bill, I found a few charges for services for $100. I could only imagine what they were. It taught me to cap the expenses of my visitors and let them know of it beforehand. It would never happen again.

It's strange . . . even many Yankee fans who showed up for his appearances had a love-hate relationship with Jackson. They loved him for his exploits on the field, but seemed to resent his arrogance and attitude. He wasn't your typical Yankee hero: unlike DiMaggio, Mantle, Rizzuto, and Berra, Jackson was anything but lovable and humble.

The best Reggie story I can relate is a report from *Sports Collectors Digest*. After Reggie had concluded his career, he was sitting in the stands at a California Angels game. A woman kept asking him for autographs on two baseballs for her sons. Reggie kept delaying her. Finally, she asked one last time, telling him the family was leaving. The woman reported, Reggie took the balls and signed them, all right—"Daffy Duck" on one, "Donald Duck" on the other.

Reggie was a great player with showmanship and timing. His ego is his problem. Don't expect "Mr. Wonderful" from "Mr. October" unless you've got a cameraman nearby.

Joe DiMaggio

"Joe D" is a case of the autograph craze driving a man mad while reaping huge financial rewards. Joe DiMaggio was a great guy until the hounds finally got to him. Unfortunately, his rough demeanor carried over to paid appearances, leaving many who paid for the signature bewildered by their treatment. He was often grumpy and acted like he didn't want to be there.

The first time I met DiMaggio was in 1986 at a Washington, D.C. hotel where the athletes were staying for the Cracker Jack® All Star Game. Joe had just exited the lobby elevator and was greeted by at least 25 hounds. He signed patiently, occasionally asking for a limit of one-per-person. Only a few would obtain a second signature.

In March, 1986, "Joltin' Joe" was again a willing signer at the Italian Open golf tournament in Tampa. But over the next three years he became less cooperative and willing, using private guards who screened his way. He came to despise autograph seekers and absolutely loathed dealers. Joe often accused hounds of being dealers.

By 1989's Italian Open, Joe would only personalize items with a strict limit of one, refusing all requests once the golf began. With each paid appearance more rules were established, baffling collectors. As the number of items on his restricted list grew larger, his verbal exchange lessened with each show.

It became apparent that Joe enjoyed the money, but not the appearances. His comments could often be taken as wisecracks or sarcasm. I once saw him leave an appearance with over 50 people waiting in line when his count disagreed with the promoter's. He refused to return, even when the promoter offered to pay extra. He would never sign any photos in which Marilyn Monroe appeared.

Joe's fees rose so quickly that a $25 charge per autograph became a $150–$200 charge (depending on the item). Often he would ignore a comment and just move on to the next person. At those prices, payers felt they deserved more.

In a 1997 appearance advertisement in *Sports Collectors Digest,* a disclaimer stated that 'Mr. DiMaggio would not sign photo baseballs, custom made balls, multi-signed balls, flats larger than 16" X 20", lithographs, oil paintings, seriographs, baseball cards, Perez-Steele cards, other artwork, books, photographs unless related to baseball, albums, gloves, jerseys, or bats. Mr. DiMaggio will not sign anything other than his name.' This seemed to leave very little.

The hounds and dealers had rattled Joe. He changed from one of the nicest guys ever to a grumpy old man who came to hate the autograph industry—but the money was too good to hate it that much. It's the freebies that bothered Joe.

Pete Rose

When you're 90 minutes late for a paid appearance, then complain because you had to leave your unfinished round of golf, you're a jerk. This brings us to Pete Rose, another athlete who rubs people the wrong way.

It's my opinion that baseball's banning of Pete Rose is more a vendetta against him for his arrogant, in-your-face personality than it was for gambling. You certainly can't deny his on-the-field performances: in 1985 he was the hottest thing in sports, as he

Pete Rose is the fastest signer alive. His arrogance, not his betting, is keeping out of the Hall of Fame.
—Photo by Tom Bunevich

pursued the all-time hit record. Baseball loved him and used him to promote the sport.

Rose also got bombarded by the hounds, especially after the 1985 season, but would often grin and bear it. If he could avoid a crowd, he would. He's always been a draw at shows. His appearances are all business. Expect little feedback; it's head down, sign, do the next one, keep moving. Occasionally, he'll acknowledge your presence or remarks. Somehow, he always notices the good-looking women and exchanges conversation with them. He can offer a serious comment, then follow it with an off-color, off-the-wall remark. Rough language comes easy.

Pete does the minimum in appearances. He churns out the signatures and to his credit, they all look the same. He gets an "A" for penmanship.

Pete's past is legendary. Gambling, women, and an almost defiant personality have caused many to dislike him. He clearly isn't the All-American male; we like our heroes a little humble. Pete Rose is far from that.

Gaylord Perry

Another example of a jerk is any athlete who agrees to an appearance, then tell others he's purposely not going to show up. That's exactly what Perry did to me and the Major League Baseball Players Alumni Association (MLBPAA) in 1996.

Perry can be two different people. One is a nice guy, telling baseball war stories as though you're one of the guys. The other can just ignore you like you're not even there, or clearly indicate you are bothering him. He can become very uncooperative.

I had my first encounter with Perry at the MLBPAA's 1994 Card Fair. Perry had agreed to be a guest for the show with all proceeds going to the MLBPAA. As he prepared for his appearance, we asked him to sign the 50 items we had received in the mail. He refused, saying he would not sign any mail. This had not been stated beforehand.

Rather than go through the process of writing refunds and sending back the items unsigned, I asked people in line to get them signed and return them to me. As we always did, we placed a Post-it® Note on the back with the owner's name and address. About halfway through the items, Perry asked a customer where the items came from. Once Perry heard they were mail order items, he left the room and went into a hospitality area, asking for a ride back to the hotel. He left a crowd of about 150 people waiting for his autograph.

I went into the room, asked him to return, showed him our mail order records and pleaded with him to at least finish for those in attendance. The records clearly indicated the name, address, and item to be signed. I told him of the difficulty of refunds, and that we wouldn't have taken mail order items if we had known beforehand that he would not sign them.

Perturbed, he finished for the public, then signed the remaining mail items for me. He accepted my apologies and left. Although my actions may have been wrong, I felt changing the rules forced me to try drastic measures.

In 1995, I ran into Perry at a show at the Ted Williams Museum in Hernando, Florida, where we both went about our business as if nothing had happened. At that time, I thought everything was okay.

In 1996, Perry agreed to do an appearance for the MLBPAA for a small fee as one of our Sunday headliners. Rumors flew that he was not going to show for his 11 a.m. to 1 p.m. appearance. When he had not shown by noon I offered refunds to the 200 playing customers, many of whom had driven for three or four hours. I could only apologize.

I felt badly for those who had come. Perry may have had his revenge on me, but he also penalized those who came to see him.

I'd rather have had him smack me in the face than to do that to these innocent people.

Now you know why he got traded so much. Others must have seen the jerk in Gaylord Perry.

Denny McLain

I've had Denny at two appearances, and haven't had much trouble with him. However, I've seen a side of him that comes off as a smart aleck, know-it-all who thinks he can do no wrong. His brushes with the law and the many new chances he's been given indicate he believes he's clearly above society's rules.

Denny is a smooth talker who knows when to turn on the charm. He also will offer his opinion on any subject and tell you exactly the way he sees it. I've seen him be short with people at times, but never at a paid appearance. There, he's usually on better behavior.

Other promoters have reported experiences with an uncooperative McLain. They felt shortchanged, either in time or the number of autographs. I've often thought Denny misbehaves just to see what he can get away with. Unfortunately, it's always catching up with him.

Denny was on top of the world in 1968 as MVP with the Cy Young Award, a 31-6 record, and the World Series Championship. He would later do jail time and always seemed to be in trouble. With all the chances he's been given, you'd think he'd have learned. Instead, Denny McLain became the poster boy for today's spoiled athlete. I'm afraid he's finally run out of chances.

Well, so much for jerks. Let's turn the page and talk about some good guys.

Chapter 5

My Top Ten Good Guys

Based on personal experiences, interviews with promoters and autograph collectors and hounds, here are my Top Ten Good Guys:

1. Brooks Robinson
2. Harmon Killebrew
3. Lee Roy Selmon
4. Otto Graham
5. The Famous Chicken
6. Monte Irvin
7. Billy Williams
8. Muhammad Ali
9. Bobby Hull
10. tie: Alan Trammell and Dale Murphy

Brooks Robinson

God invented the perfect card show guest when He made Brooks Robinson. He's the perfect blend of everything a card show guest should be—friendly, polite, courteous, talkative, and engaging —all while maintaining a quick signing pace.

Brooks Robinson, with sons Matt and Andrew. My number one nice guy, the perfect card show guest.
—Photo by Joanne Thresher

Having hosted Brooks at least six times and seeing him countless other times, I've never heard him raise his voice, refuse a request, or fail to converse. He'll take the time to make you feel glad you asked him for an autograph.

Brooks handles items with care, always double-checking with your request when you ask for more than an autograph. His signature will always look the same. I've seen him charm the kids and ladies, and he almost always thanks the requestor for coming. At the end of every session, he's always doubled-checked with me to see that he's completely finished. I once had a mail request for 17 items to be listed on a baseball and Brooks not only took his time doing them, he re-checked them.

I've seen Brooks remember faces and sometimes even names from shows the year before. He's got an incredible memory.

Brooks Robinson has a southern, down home friendliness that lets you believe he's enjoying himself. He knows autographs are part of the price for fame, but he's learned to enjoy the moment. He's got class.

Harmon Killebrew

Killebrew is much like Brooks Robinson in autograph appearances. He's cooperative, pleasant, friendly, courteous, and engaging. He truly enjoys spending time with the fans, so much that he tends to move at a slow signing pace. Promoters should make sure they have Harmon on a per-piece method, since his attention is so focused on the person asking for the autograph. He's slow and deliberate, handling each piece with care.

Killebrew is a member of the 500 career home run club, leaving him more of a subject for autograph hounds. He almost always signs in crowded situations, although he asks a limit of one-per-person. Consistency in the quality of his signature is another trademark. It will always look the same.

Once you're a friend with Killebrew, he'll remember you and he'll even go out of his way to acknowledge your presence. His concern is genuine. He's sort of a softer-spoken Brooks Robinson.

One difference between Harmon and Brooks is that Killebrew is more concerned with the business end of things. You could tell Brooks he has ten hours left and he'd say, "Just tell me when I'm done." Killebrew will ask you what number you're on and when his time is up. He's just more on top of things.

Killebrew's got class—definitely the most of all the 500 home run club members. He enjoys the limelight, but keeps it on a personal basis between him and the autograph collector.

Lee Roy Selmon

I've never heard a bad word about Lee Roy Selmon. He's easily the most modest professional athlete I've ever met. Sometimes, he is even taken aback by the adulation and attention.

Lee Roy is treated like a god in Tampa with justification. He's done so much in the community and for local charities and other good causes that I think he can't say "no." When he was elected into the Pro Football Hall of Fame, the requests for autographs for the former Buccaneer were overwhelming, but he always took the time to sign. At one of my appearances, he stayed thirty minutes over on his own time to fulfill all requests.

Lee Roy is basically quiet, and more of a listener than a talker. He'll take his time to sign the items and listen to all the stories and requests.

I think Lee Roy is one of those guys who wonders what the commotion is all about. Sometimes I think the constant bombardment bothers him, but he just keeps signing away. Lee Roy lives his strong Christian beliefs. He doesn't preach it, but he shows it in the way he lives. You'll never hear him criticize others—that's not his style.

After you've known Lee Roy for a while, you wonder how this guy could be the same great hard-nosed, aggressive player that dominated the NFL in 1979. He wasn't the kind for dirty play or talking trash. Instead, he just played hard. He's truly a gentle giant off the field, and a super nice guy.

Otto Graham

Otto Graham with Sue, Matt and me. Women should expect a kiss from Otto, another member of my Top Ten Good Guys.—Photo by Joanne Thresher

Around other guys, Otto fits in as one of the guys. He loves to tell stories and listen to yours. If you're a woman asking for an autograph, chances are he'll offer a good kiss on the cheek.

His memory is sharp. He'll look at old photos and tell you the time and place they were taken. He'll provide the details for specific plays, games, and events. The best part is that he is willing to share them with you.

Besides his warmth, he'll oblige with a clean, quality signature every time. I've seen hounds hand him multiple items in crowded situations and he signs them all. Like Selmon, he rarely criticizes, although the theatrics and antics of today's athletes—like celebrations, hotdogging and playing to the crowd—bother him. He's quick to tell you that in his day, that wasn't part of the game.

Call Otto for a charity function and chances are he'll say, "yes." He just likes being around people. People bring out the best in him—a bubbly, happy, pleasant personality. He'll take his time with each and every person, making sure everyone is happy. His slow speed allows for prolonged conversation and exchange. Otto doesn't worry about the time. He told me once during an appearance when I reminded him we were running out of time that "It doesn't matter, I'll stay as long as there is still a person that wants an autograph."

Knowing him as I do, he'd stay 12 hours if he had to and not complain once, especially if you got him started telling his war stories.

The Famous Chicken

"Fun" is the best word to describe The Famous Chicken. If you see The Chicken perform you will see the funniest mascot ever. After his appearances, he takes time to sign autographs for all those that want them. He won't sign while performing but it's worth the wait.

The Chicken will personalize, pose, joke, converse, and make sure you've had a good time. He's in no hurry, and will stay as long as required. He also carries items you can get signed

The Famous Chicken and me. World's best mascot. He might be tremendous with kids but he still couldn't tell me which came first—the chicken or the egg. —Photo by Joanne Thresher

such as photos, dolls, and other memorabilia, all at reasonable prices. There's never a charge for an autograph, and The Chicken always provides a neat, clear signature.

In his sit-down appearances, you never can tell when The Chicken might do the unexpected, such as "attack" a youngster, jump across the table and kiss a female, or act like he's sleeping when someone's taking a long time with a camera. It's always in good fun.

In one of his three-hour appearances with me, he was still going 90 miles an hour in the last few minutes. Afterward, I saw him enjoying pizza and a soft drink, the head and upper body portion of his costume removed and his t-shirt soaked with sweat. He enjoys what he's doing and works hard at it.

In going to the source to ask him which came first, The Chicken or the egg, I couldn't get an answer, as he didn't know. One guarantee about this Chicken—you'll never see him in (pardon the pun) a fowl mood. He's the best.

Monte Irvin

Monte Irvin. This Baseball Hall of Famer is one my Ten Good Guys and a good friend.
—Photo by Joanne Thresher

This baseball Hall of Famer can be described as a true gentleman. I've known Monte for 16 years and he's always been cooperative, pleasant, friendly, and polite. Age has slowed him and given him some health problems, but his personality hasn't changed.

Perhaps because he played mostly in the Negro Leagues and only for eight seasons in the majors, Irvin is one of the least known of all Hall of Famers and many times blends in with the crowd. When approached in public he will accommodate all requests, but often with limits on the number.

In public appearances Monte is genuine, taking time to acknowledge those who came, conversing and happy to go the extra mile for photographs and personalizations. Monte always gives a neat, clean autograph. He will also answer his mail, although he's not as quick as he used to be.

Monte's not a war storyteller. He'll talk about anything, although he's not forceful with his opinions. He's soft-spoken, preferring to add his two cents as a matter of fact. His memory is keen and he remembers faces well, though not necessarily names. He can recall details of many moments in his career.

Interestingly, Monte was Willie Mays's roommate for a period in the 1950s when both played for the New York Giants. They're still friends, although Monte acknowledges that Mays's generally erratic behavior at appearances baffles him.

"I don't know, Tom," he once told me. "He wasn't like that when he played."

Monte lives the slower-paced retired life in Homosassa Springs, Florida. His family is important to him, and he always asks about my wife and two children. Since he was also a black player in the 1950s, one might wonder if there's any bitterness. Monte lets you know it surely existed, but that he has moved on.

Roy Campanella called Irvin upon Monte's induction in the Hall of Fame, "the greatest all around player I ever saw." Irvin has never received his due. But in his inimitable style he'll never complain; he's got too much class to do so.

Billy Williams

In my mind, I pictured Williams as a tough, uncooperative, distant cookie. The exact opposite is true. If "nice guys finish last," as Leo Durocher once said, then it's no wonder the Chicago Cubs won't make him manager; they'd never win.

Williams came dressed for my first appearance with him in a three-piece suit. Most athletes wear neat, casual clothing, such as golf attire. He told me he wanted to make a good impression for everyone attending the signing.

This Cub great is friendly, cooperative, and welcomes personalizations and photographs. He's in no hurry, always pausing to converse with the fans, even if he's the one who initiates the small talk. He's glad to discuss baseball, but doesn't get carried away.

His signature is among the sloppiest in sports, but it always looks the same. He'll never win any penmanship awards. In public, he'll sign autographs on his time (usually limiting to one) and shows a preference for children. He'll acknowledge that hounds can be pests, but acknowledges that they also are part of the cost of popularity. Billy is another who remembers faces and places of those he's met before, sometimes even pulling out the right names.

Williams enjoys a good laugh, especially when it's something humorous relating to his baseball career. He's not caught up in the game of days gone by; he'd almost prefer to talk about his family. He seems to live by the old adage, "speak when you're spoken to," since his quiet nature defines him and his career.

When he does talk, he does himself proud. "Sweet Swing Billy," as he was called in his playing days, is a sweetheart.

Muhammad Ali

Despite his worldwide acclaim, Muhammad Ali has remained a "people person." He still exhibits character traits that leave the impression he is indeed "The Greatest," whether you were a fan or not.

Illness has taken a toll on his body, but his mind is sharp. He hears your words and acknowledges them with a smile, head bob, raise of the eyebrow, or a handshake. His motor skills have been affected by Parkinson's disease, he writes slowly, but takes his time to make it clean and consistent. He can only do about 600 autographs in a five hour period, but the last one will look like the first.

Unfortunately, free autographs from Ali are difficult. He always has security personnel around. If he starts signing, it turns into a mob scene. He does answer his mail, although it can take up to two years for a reply. The best way to get Ali's autograph is at a show appearance; however, the fee is usually in the $90–$150 range, depending on the item. He makes three or four such appearances per year. Because writing is such a chore, he limits personalizations and extra notations. Once you see him struggling to give his best, you can't feel offended.

During your time with Ali, he'll be glad to pose for photographs. In fact, he'll often invite you behind the table and stand with you. He'll limit conversations, but body gestures provide the answers. He'll often smile and break into his patented body stance. He's not interested in a speedy autograph session; he'd rather have you leave happy and satisfied. This is one legend who can still turn on the charm.

Ali was probably the greatest athlete in using the media to forge an image of the loud, boisterous, and arrogantly over- confident athlete. When you spend a few minutes with him, you see a modesty and humility that tell you, "That was all an act; this is the real me . . . the kinder, gentler man."

On rare occasions, he'll sign his original name of Cassius Clay. In the estimated 3,000 autographs I've seen him sign, I saw him pen the Clay name only once. It was on an Olympic boxing photo and was given only after many repeated requests and an assurance it was not for re-sale.

Ali was a king in the ring, and also a champ out of it.

Bobby Hull

When you think of hockey players, you envision rough and tough personalities. With Bobby Hull, you get a someone who displays those playing traits, but also a man who might best be described as your golfing buddy at the country club. He's just one of the guys.

In public, Hull is usually seen sporting a smiling, friendly attitude. He's a willing signer, but limits the number per person in crowded situations. He's always willing to personalize, pose, and participate, and his signature is one of the neatest and most consistent of all. You can always count on Bobby for cooperation.

Hull likes to joke, also, and occasionally will provide an offbeat story. He sometimes refers to himself as Brett Hull's dad (current NHL star). He loves the game of hockey and always pumps up the sport in glowing terms. He's not a hurried signer, but prefers to spend time with each person, and will often ask questions to get the ball rolling. A Chicago icon, he loves talking about his days as a Blackhawk, although not in any way that makes him come across as a braggart.

Bobby went the extra mile for me, staying overtime to sign a number of leftover pictures when he realized the crowd had come up short in covering his fee. He's got a youthful face, tailored hair look, and a still-impressive physique that makes him look younger than his years.

Hull has a bit of a rough vocabulary; after all, he's a hockey player. Other than that Bobby's one cool dude and he always seems to be enjoying himself.

Alan Trammell

Trammell was a shortstop for the Detroit Tigers from the late 70s through the mid-90s. He does few appearances today, but was always a willing signer in his days when the Tigers were spring training in Florida.

His personality mirrors the way he played. He was quiet, unassuming and went about his job with little fanfare. I've witnessed him be the only player to stop for an autograph when several players were making their way from the parking lot to the locker room. He'll personalize, pose for photographs, and even engage in conversation, but you'll have to lead the discussion; he won't say much. In crowded situations he'll sign for all, but limit autographs to one each.

Alan was a willing signer before and after games, and whenever the chance presented itself. He was an athlete who realized that signing goes with the territory, and decided to just do it with no excuses. In at least 10 encounters with him I never saw him refuse an autograph request, unless it was on the field when he had other business on his mind. He also signs through the mail.

Trammell has borderline Hall of Fame credentials, but because of his quiet nature he'll never receive proper credit and will probably never be voted into baseball's shrine. Hounds will tell you he does belong in the Good Guy Hall Of Fame.

Dale Murphy

If the Atlanta Braves were America's team in the 1980s, Murphy was America's player. Murphy has refused to do paid appearances even for charities, since a fee would be attached to the signing. He does answer mail, although it has been known to take as long as six months. He's another who never refuses an autograph request.

Murphy is well-mannered and courteous, willing to please with personalizations and photo requests, often signing multiple items. Dale limits requests to one-per-person in larger crowds to accommodate as many as possible.

I once saw Murphy standing along an outfield fence signing autographs *after* play had begun in a spring training game. He stayed almost an inning to meet the demand. At a hotel I saw him sign a dozen items and pose for a few photographs with a 12-year-old who said he was a big fan. Murphy made that awestruck kid feel like a million bucks.

Generally, Murphy is quiet and won't say much. In his prime he was a constant target for autograph seekers, but never lost his composure or refused to sign; he realized it was just part of the deal. He's not a joker or storyteller and is almost strictly business, though he's partial to kids and they always get preferential treatment. You can sometimes tell that the pushy adult hounds bother him, but he just bites his lip and keeps on signing.

This one guy who doesn't subscribe to Murphy's Law— whatever can go wrong will go wrong. Instead, he's what is right with hero worship; a real All-American guy.

Now it's on to much more about 100 famous athletes.

Tom Bunevich

Chapter 6

Rating Another 100 Well-Known Sports Celebrities

Based on personal experiences, interviews with promoters, autograph collectors, and hounds, here's how I see the following 100 well-known sports celebrities.

Hank Aaron

Hank is a "let's get this over with" type guy. He's not going to talk much, and will sign rapidly and keep things moving. He's not a storyteller and doesn't like to do personalizations and photos, as they consume time.

Aaron will make an attempt to avoid the crowds. He will refuse many times in crowded situations, and when he does sign, it's usually on the run. Don't expect to have your mail returned either.

Hank's signature has been deteriorating in recent years. He says he

Hank Aaron with the family. Hank seems to just want to get it over with, but usually draws large crowds—Photo by Joanne Thresher

has arthritis in his hand. In the high-speed world of appearances, he is a huge draw as the all-time home run king. His signature worsens as he signs. He'll converse but expect short, quick, and sometimes even sarcastic answers.

Aaron keeps to himself and is never going to win you over with kindness. His personality is more one of tolerance than friendliness. The years of fame and constant hounding have taken their toll. You almost think he'd rather be left alone.

Luis Aparicio

Aparicio is a true gentleman. Friendly, courteous, and cooperative, he welcomes personalizations, photos, and conversation. His aim is to please. Luis's signature is always consistent, neat and never hurried. Sometimes because of his trouble with the English language, you have to spell things for him.

Luis will talk, but you have to initiate the conversation. He's got great recall about incidents in his career. He's a straight shooter though, and won't jazz up the story. He likes to have fun, but signing is serious to him. His gentlemanly nature prevents him from losing his cool. You won't see him angry or hear negative talk.

In crowded situations, he's a great signer but limits the number. Since he lives out of the country, don't expect him to return mail. Your best bet is a show appearance, although he doesn't do many.

He's a Latin American hero for his baseball exploits. They picked a fine man to honor.

Bert Blyleven

Bert is a fun-loving guy who can show a nasty side, and has come to despise autograph hounds. He will only personalize autographs, unless it is a special item that needs his signature to be complete, like a team ball. He'll tell you he hates the entire autograph scene, and strictly limits signatures to one each when in public. Forget the mail; he's not going to return it.

His signature is consistently sloppy. He won't say much, and you have to force the conversation. I think he doesn't care what you think of him—he's going to be himself, even if it means being short with you or refusing photographs or other requests. When not in an autograph environment, Bert is friendly and just blends in as one of the guys. Just keep the pens and Sharpies® away when you're with Bert and you'll do fine. Bring them out, and you'll see a changed man.

Gary Carter

Carter is a genuinely nice guy who treats autograph collectors with dignity and class. He'll accommodate special or photo requests, and go out of his way to make sure you're happy. He'll talk baseball, family, politics, sports—anything you want to talk about. He's not in a hurry, although his poor penmanship looks like it's always the case.

However, Gary will not sign baseball cards unless the requestor makes a $25 donation to the Leukemia Society. This is to honor a vow he made to the agency to raise funds in his mother's name; she passed away from the disease when Gary was a youngster. Many times collectors get mad, not knowing this beforehand. After he explains the situation, he even offers information on the process to get cards signed. He'll gladly autograph any other item.

When he played, Carter was quiet and did most of his talking on the field. He'll discuss his moments in baseball, but he won't jazz up the stories. He's actually a bit shy, and sometimes, I think he's embarrassed by all the attention. All in all, Gary's much the same at all times. His cooperation, courtesy, and good guy qualities are part of Carter's make-up. It won't smother you—but it does leave a good impression of "The Kid."

Carlton Fisk

Carlton shows his emotions well. Often, his actions—like walking out of a signing session when he's angry—speak louder than words. Carlton can be two different people—the nicest guy imaginable, or the meanest man in the world. A hint: if he taps his writing instrument, he's angry.

I've seen Fisk carry on conversations with strangers during signings for five minutes or more, apparently enjoying himself. I've also seen him ignore a question and shove a person's item away wildly while reaching for the next to be signed. He'll never win you with kindness, that's not his style.

The other side of Fisk? Both times I hosted him as a guest he donated all fees to charity, resulting in over $20,000 for two causes. Yet, I've seen him be more personable when he's getting the appearance fee. Forget the mail route—it won't come back. Carlton's real problem is with dealers who have profited at his expense. He's won't stay much, and there will usually be short answers to your questions. Don't even think about a second freebie, as Fisk usually refuses additional requests. He'll do personalizations and photos when it's not crowded, but don't count on them in appearances.

Carlton's personality is much like the one he displayed in his career: all business, with little time for fun and games. He did things hard, but did them his way. He still lives like that, and his mood will determine your opinion. He can be both a good guy and a jerk within the same ten minutes; with him, you never know. Be alert.

Bob Gibson

Bob Gibson can be two different people. When doing a paid appearance he's courteous, friendly, cooperative and talkative. In a non-paid situation he's just the opposite, and has little trouble saying no to autograph requests.

In paid appearances, Gibson understands that personalizations, photographs and conversation are part of the deal. He'll gladly talk baseball and about himself, generally giving you short, direct answers. He won't mince words and will tackle controversial subjects with his honest opinion. He might suggest a certain player is overrated, or that another is not a team player—and will stand behind his statements. In the past, Bob has been vocal about the blacks in baseball's leadership. Try to remember that he lived it and is probably one of those guys with a chip still on his shoulder. Don't expect to have mail requests returned: Bob's actions and constant refusals let you know he's not crazy about the whole autograph scene, unless pay is involved.

Gibson will reveal that during his career he had extreme confidence in his abilities, a fierce competitive nature, and an attitude that sometimes rubs others the wrong way. He still has those qualities. In any case, don't expect a kind, fun-loving guy; Bob's serious nature doesn't lend itself to many laughs.

There's little question that Gibson enjoys the money associated with autograph appearances. To his credit, his actions, behavior and attitude at such showings leave a positive impression. At other times, you'll likely be disappointed.

Rod Carew

Carew is quiet, soft-spoken and unassuming. He's shy by nature and not much of a talker. In paid appearances he's cooperative, friendly, and courteous. In public, he'll often refuse autograph requests, but much depends on crowd size. Forget mail— he's not going to answer it.

Carew comes off as a bland personality. If he won the lottery, I don't think he'd show much excitement. He has an intellectual quality that reveals more of the thinker than a doer in conversations. Rod will think before he speaks or acts; if you want conversation, you're going to have to start (and prolong) it.

I believe that after years in the public eye, Carew just prefers to be alone. He's in his own little world. He's not mean or spiteful, although its evident that the hounds annoy him with their constant requests. He plays the game at his paid appearances of being the nice guy, although it's obvious he'd rather be somewhere else. Rod Carew is in the middle: you won't be overwhelmed at meeting him, but at the same time you'll wish there was more. What you see is what you get.

Steve Carlton

Carlton is much like Bob Gibson: two different people at paid appearances as opposed to being out in public. However, Steve's change is more radical. I asked him for autographs numerous times in Clearwater for the Phillies' spring training and was refused every time. Many times, he just ignored me.

At paid appearances, Carlton is Mr. Nice Guy. He'll personalize, pose, joke, converse, and be mannerly. At charitable events he'll usually exhibit better behavior, but will limit the autographs. In a non-paid situation, expect to be turned down, even if you are alone; he just doesn't sign for free. Mail requests usually go unanswered. When I inquired about his constant refusals, he got defensive.

"I'm going to work, and I didn't sign when I was working," Carlton told me. "It was nothing personal; I regarded that as my time. I didn't bother you when *you* were working."

Steve can speak on any subject and won't shy away from an honest opinion. He seems knowledgeable on many subjects. I personally believe he cares little what you think of him. He's going to be himself, whether it leaves a positive or negative impression. He's not going to fake it, and won't mind telling you when he's annoyed. There's little to dislike with the paid-appearance Carlton, but avoid the other one; he won't win any nice guy prizes there.

Hank Bauer

Bauer was one of Mickey Mantle's closest friends and sidekicks. Hank is a super-nice guy, regardless if it's a paid, charitable, or public appearance. You always get a friendly, cooperative, fun-loving guy willing to go the extra mile with photos, personalizations and conversation.

Hank loves the war stories, and jazzes them up with a great storytelling ability. Hank's from the old school, though; he has opinions about every subject. Listening to him, you're convinced it was always better in the olden days. He'll answer his mail, but he's in no hurry to get it out. The signature is always clean, neat and consistent.

Bauer often just blends in as one of the older guys. He remembers faces and places from those he's met previously. He's got a genuine, good nature about him that makes him easy to like. Although the haircut provides the tough military look, don't be fooled: he's really easy going.

Catfish Hunter

Catfish Hunter possessed Southern charm with all the attributes of a gentleman. On the shy and quiet side, he wouldn't waste words and spoke when spoken to. In public or show appearances, he'd go beyond the call to please. He'd personalize, pose, and converse, always showing courtesy and respect.

Sometimes you could tell that the hounds were abusing him with multiple requests, but he'd grin and bear it. Hunter

Jim "Catfish" Hunter with Andrew and Matt. A truly quiet guy who's early death proved that the good do sometimes die young.—Photo by Joanne Thresher

was given the name "Catfish" by former A's owner Charlie Finley because of his North Carolina farm background. It fit Jim well, who wasn't a storyteller and into deep conversation; he was more content to just lay back and take it all in.

From poor farm boy to rich free agent pitcher to the Hall of Fame, Hunter didn't change much. He was still the polite, modest, and accommodating athlete that didn't let fame go to his head. Perhaps it was the life on the farm that kept his feet on the ground and made him a very likable guy.

Ernie Banks

"Mr. Cub" overwhelms you with his friendliness, courtesy and attitude, but he's a promoter's nightmare. He goes slowly, spending a lot of time with each person and getting involved in lengthy conversations.

He takes time to sing, stretch, stand for photographs and even act out his baseball heroics. Ernie will strike up a conversation like he's your everyday friend. If you get him talking, you may have to end the conversation in order to escape. That's why he often gets in trouble with promoters for producing so few autographs in his time period.

Banks is a lovable guy who always seems to see the fun in things. He'll gladly sign as asked, and most of the time includes "Peace, Love, Happiness" with his autograph. Forget the mail, though: Ernie's not going to sign that route. His wife carries the weight in negotiations, and she can be a tough cookie. In non-paid appearances, Ernie has much the same attitude and behavior.

What impresses you about Ernie is that he will remember you from previous appearances if you've spent any time with him. He's not good at names, but faces ring a bell. Even though a good guy like Banks never got an opportunity to play in a World Series, he'll tell you he's not bothered by it. "I still have lots of great memories," he once told me, "but I'm really goin' to enjoy it when the Cubs win a World Series."

You'll rarely see Banks without a smile. There's little to dislike about him.

Lou Brock

The first time I hosted Brock he arrived in a suit and tie, wanting to make a solid impression, which he did with his friendliness, courtesy, and cooperation. Lou is on the shy side, but once he loosens up, he'll converse freely about any subject. He'll laugh, but he's not a joker or cut-up. He's more serious than comic.

Brock is a modest man who dislikes talking about himself. He's friendly, polite, and cooperative. Even in public he'll sign, but usually limits the number per person. His recall of specifics for incidents in his playing career is incredible; he can tell you all about counts, places, opponents, pitchers, etc.

You won't hear Lou crying the blues about the treatment blacks received during his early playing days. He'll talk about it if forced, but it's just not his style to be negative. You usually will see him smiling away, cheerful and willing to talk.

Brock probably never received the credit he deserved since he played in St. Louis—not exactly a media hotbed. Even when Henderson broke his career stolen base record, Brock was seen smiling, congratulating Rickey and enjoying the moment for both baseball greats.

I don't think Lou's a glory hound—he just wants to know he did his job well.

Ray Dandridge

I got to know Ray quite well in the last two years before his death, hosting him in four signings during that period. This was a whale of a guy who never had a negative word. He was also one of those guys who's just naturally funny.

Ray made his name as a Negro League star in the 1930s and 1940s, and never got an opportunity to play in the majors. He told me he regretted that chance, but understood that it wasn't going to happen in his day. There was no bitterness.

Dandridge was friendly, accommodating, courteous, and witty. He never refused an autograph request, or the opportunity to go the extra mile. He was happy to personalize, pose or converse, was never in a hurry, and never seemed to get rattled.

Ray had amazing recall about his playing career, but couldn't tell you what he ate for breakfast yesterday. He spoke softly and carried himself with a modesty that made it hard to believe this was a Hall of Fame player. He always made you feel welcome and could converse for hours, especially with his tales of the Negro League greats.

As I watched Ray's health decline and death come closer, I saw a man die with dignity who never bemoaned his fate. Instead, he spoke about how lucky he was to have lived the life he did. I continually chided him for smoking, and I'm afraid it took its toll. I miss Ray, but every time I think of him, I smile. He was a good man.

Bob Feller

I have known Bob Feller since 1985 and have watched him change from an accommodating, likable guy to present-day grouch. Bob is a guy whose bark is worse than his bite. He'll often act as though he's not going to sign, but will sign while growling about it.

He's full of baseball stories, and will tell you about how good it was in the "olden days," and how today's athletes are pampered and not as tough as those he knew. He'll converse about any subject, but over the years has become more negative and cynical.

Bob complains about photos and personalizations, but ends up doing them. He'll answer his mail and will take time to sign in public. Once upon a time he signed freely and rarely limited the freebies. Now, there are limits.

Feller catches a lot of heat for the large number of appearances he's made through the years. To him, it was a chance to make a buck. To his credit, he kept his fees reasonable and never complained about how long he had to stay.

Bob still is fan-friendly, but over the years the hounds have toughen him up, making him complain and moan more often.

Don Drysdale

Don was a friendly, polite man who understood his place in the limelight, but wasn't enamored with it. He said little, despite a Hall of Fame baseball and broadcasting career. You almost had to force the conversation.

After he was elected to the Hall of Fame, Drysdale became a tougher autograph. He learned to avoid the crowds and limit the numbers. In appearances, he accommodated all requests for personalizations and photographs. He moved slowly, making sure each was a clean, quality autograph. While inviting conversation, he didn't waste words and wasn't wrapped in stories of the old days. Though answering mail autograph requests he was in no hurry to return them, being known to take as along as six months.

Don fit the Dodger hero of the 1950s and 60s mold—speak softly, display class, and realize you have an obligation to the public. This also meant you kept your distance. He was never going to be the life of the party. He seemed to prefer peace and quiet.

Rollie Fingers

Fingers is the wittiest athlete I've ever met, capable of making a wisecrack in a straight-faced manner that leaves you rolling in laughter. He's courteous, friendly, accommodating, and willing to go the extra mile for autograph seekers. Rollie reminds you of the Alfred E. Neuman of *Mad Magazine* fame: "What—me worry?"

Rollie can change moods from loud, fun-loving cutup to serious conversationalist in a heartbeat. When he tells a baseball war story, he jazzes it up for all the details and somehow always manages to make it funny. At other times, Fingers just seems like he's part of the scenery.

Forget the mail route, as some requests will be returned while others go unanswered. Rollie will sign in public, but limits individual numbers. In all cases, he takes the time to provide a clean, quality signature.

Once during an appearance where Fingers and Mays were joined by six or seven other signers in a crowded tent, Rollie gave me one of his perfectly-timed lines. I was standing on a table

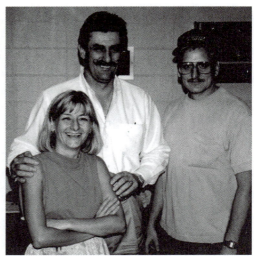

Rollie Fingers with Sue and me. His sense of humor, even in chaotic times, cracks you up.—Photo by Joanne Thresher

shouting, that "persons with Willie Mays tickets should line up right here." I heard Fingers say in a deadpan voice in the background, "I think he wants everybody in the Willie Mays line to line up there." I burst out laughing, enjoying the much-needed comic relief.

Rollie had such an ease about him that it was easy to understand his success as a relief pitcher. He just marched along—sometimes to his own drummer. However, you'll never see him lose his cool. "What—me worry?"

Whitey Ford

Whitey is as friendly a guy as you'll find on the card show circuit, but can be a toughie in public, especially in larger demanding crowds. He's cooperative, smiling, and aims to please when it's a paid deal. You can expect personalizations and photographs in such appearances, but in public, the crowd determines your fate and Ford's degree of cooperation.

Ford keeps his mind on more than the signing, with an eye on the number signed or time remaining. He says he's been taken advantage of by promoters, so he pays more attention to such details now.

Whitey loves the stories, especially those about the old Yankees and Mickey Mantle. He'll converse with autograph seekers, and return compliments with his own kind comments. A few years back Ford went through a cancer scare, and has since limited his appearances. The mail route will produce little return.

Through the years as the hounds have attacked him, Ford has gotten better at avoiding the crowds. But appearances are all positive, as Ford turns on the charm. He's got a quick wit, likes to laugh and truly shows why he was known as "Chairman of the Board."

Rick Ferrell

When I hosted Ferrell, he was 88 years of age—the oldest living baseball Hall of Famer. Although he moved slowly and the mind took awhile to recall, he was a true gentleman. He made sure each signature received his best treatment, despite his shakiness.

He didn't joke much, as he was a serious conversationalist. He would exchange banter with the fans, but always aimed to please. There was a calm about him that seemed to suggest that all things would work out as they should.

A boxer in his younger days, his personality suggested the opposite. He seemed to be easygoing and soft-spoken. Before his death, he made a habit of returning mail and enjoyed the adulation that the Hall of Fame brought to him, even at such a late time in life.

Ferrell played in the 1930s and 40s and represented the motto of many players of that era—"Do your talking on the field." It was obvious he lived by that motto.

Andre Dawson

Dawson is a quiet, soft-spoken man of few words, but accommodating, courteous, and polite.

I hosted Dawson the day it was announced he had lost an arbitration hearing. To his credit, he shrugged off the bad news and treated those who came for an autograph with kindness and cooperation.

Dawson's not a storyteller, and doesn't get into speaking about his heroics. He has modesty that shows in his actions and speech. He answers mail and is a willing signer in public. It seems that it is easier for Andre to just sign than to walk away or refuse requests. He clearly understands that he has a duty to the public and sees that it is done. His signature looks like it reads, "Alfie Clawson."

Johnny Bench

Bench is another one with different personalities in paid and unpaid appearances. In paid situations he's a gem—personable, cooperative, an overall "Mr. Nice Guy." In public, especially at golf events, Bench has no trouble refusing autograph requests. Forget the mail and hope for a good day when it's not a paid stint.

Bench agrees to personalizations, photographs, conversations and will even spin a few short baseball war stories at paid appearances. When he does sign in public, he'll offer little other than the autograph and will often make a sarcastic remark about selling the item and pocketing the profit.

Two other notable items about Bench. Umpire Al Barlick once told me Bench was among the catchers who always seem to cry most about ball and strike calls. Also, after one appearance with me, Bench bought a number of Power Ranger toys for his son from one of my dealers, spending almost $400. At the time the toys were hot items, often selling for well over the original retail value. Bench walking through the mall and later the airport with a bag full of Power Ranger toys must have been quite a sight.

Bench dislikes autograph hounds and has little trouble letting them know. However, paying for the signature assures you of a kind, gentler Johnny.

Yogi Berra

Yogi Berra always signs his name the same size regardless of the size of the item.—Photo by Joanne Thresher

One pictures Yogi as the funnyman or class clown because of all the quotes attributed to him, but it isn't so. Berra is a quiet, soft-spoken man who really doesn't say much. He'll even deny much that has been attributed to him.

Yogi does not like to personalize in appearances, using the logic that "if one wants it, they all will." He'll converse, but provide short answers and is not the storyteller that you think he'd be. There's more seriousness to do the job than to joke and converse. He'll watch the clock and try to keep a steady pace, as though he simply wants the session over with.

In public, success with Yogi depends on the crowd and circumstances. He'll usually sign one item per person, but keep walking to his destination if it's a large crowd. He'll keep his mind on signing and talk very little. In smaller crowds, Yogi will stop and give each person more time and attention. Forget the mail—he doesn't answer it, saying, "It's always the same people who send all the items."

Yogi has one quirk that amuses collectors. No matter how large the item to be signed might be, Yogi's signature always stays the same size. He'll never win a penmanship award, but his sloppy autograph always looks the same and takes up the same amount of space. Yogi is clearly a case of a falsely-painted image. He's still a good guy, but more serious than funny. Perhaps that's the reason many of those quotes seemed amusing . . . he was serious when he said them.

Don Larsen

Don Larsen's fame comes from his lone achievement, which was being the only pitcher to hurl a perfect game in World Series competition. In fact, he had a losing pitching record in the majors, but he still draws crowds because of that notable feat—the perfect World Series game.

Larsen is quiet, courteous, and accommodating, but not very outgoing. He's not going to provide long answers and carry on conversations. He will talk of his playing days, but he isn't really a storyteller. He'll answer his mail and in public appearances he is a willing signer.

Don will personalize, provide dates, numbers, and pose for photographs. He seems to realize that he has been blessed to achieve such status because of his perfect game, and revels in that accomplishment.

Larsen is laid back and understands his role in public—sign, be a nice guy and do what the people ask. His method is to be slow and steady. That's probably the best two words to describe his personality.

Roger Clemens

I was lucky enough to host Clemens in a 1987 appearance after his second Cy Young winning season. . . . What a crowd he drew, and what a job he did in the appearance!

Roger Clemens with Sue, Matt and me. We sold all 850 autographs at $8 each. Tell the Rocket he can't do it and he'll prove you wrong. —Photo by Terry Kors, Sr.

He was a perfect guest in that he posed for photographs, personalized, shook hands and seemed to enjoy meeting the public. Things have changed for Clemens. He has has cut down on personal appearances over the years and developed a reputation as a tough signer. It's easy to see that he now despises the whole autograph scene, as refusals come easy.

Forget the mail. Clemens avoids the crowds and many times he just walks past the requests, not even bothering to say "no." When he does sign he makes it a strict limit of one-per-person, and many times he will refuse to sign certain items. Over the years Clemens's friendliness has been replaced by an attitude of "just leave me alone."

In spending time with Roger, I came to believe that his success was chiefly due to a dogged determination and work ethic. He seemed to be motivated by being told that he couldn't do something and would then work to prove he could, as if a fear of failure drove him. He's a storyteller, but it almost seems you have to force him to talk about baseball.

Clemens is a future Hall of Famer. However his demeanor keeps him from increased popularity, as he values his privacy and can live without the acclaim. He first appeared with me as a youngster. Today, he's a tougher guy who doesn't seem interested in what the public thinks, and it shows.

Barry Bonds

If you approach Bonds on a good day you'll get an autograph, but on the wrong day you'll be ignored. Much depends on the size of the crowd. Forget personalizations, photos, and much conversation in either case, as Bonds is going to do the minimum. It's 50-50 on the signing potential.

Bonds does few paid appearances. At one, he put on headphones, just sign the items handed him, and virtually ignored those in attendance. Attendees felt insulted. He's not friendly by nature and keeps his distance. He will usually refuse autographs at hotels, saying it's not the place for signing. Again it's 50-50.

Barry seems to go about his business as a loner. He really doesn't seem to care what the public thinks of him, and views autographs as just part of the fame. Forget the mail route, as you'll never get your items returned. The signature, although consistent, almost seems to look like he signed in Chinese.

As a Pirates fan, I have a great appreciation for Bonds the player, but his off-the-field attitude needs a lot of work. I've seen his jerk side and his kind side—such as when he held up a youngster for a photograph. Just like on the field, he's unpredictable—but odds are you'll see more jerk than good guy.

Bobby Bonilla

Bonilla and Bonds have similar personalities, although Bonilla is certainly much more vocal. He won't mind telling you that he's not signing your item, rather than just ignoring you.

Bonilla often varies his signature, and will even give you scribbles when in crowded situations. He's more likely to refuse than sign, even in one-on-one opportunities. He hasn't done many show appearances and doesn't return mail, so you just have to be persistent and hope for a positive response if you want him to sign.

Bobby will converse, but provides short answers. Sometimes, he just seems rude and provides what seems like a smart answer. Bobby's going to be himself and not put on a false face; unfortunately many times it's an ugly one.

Bobby Doerr

Doerr received strong consideration for my Top Ten Good Guys list. He is friendly, courteous, accommodating—and most importantly, takes time to insure that you are satisfied with his efforts.

At both public and private appearances, Doerr loves to mingle with the fans. He's not a storyteller, but gladly answers baseball questions. Although he's up in years, his memory is sharp and he's still able to provide details from his career. He displays a modesty that always seems to credit others.

He'll answer mail, and is glad to sign in public. He almost seems to feel honored when you ask him for an autograph. He'll take his time providing a clean, quality signature, and the first will look just like number 500. Even in the rowdiest scenes Doerr will keep his cool and handle the situation with dignity.

Doerr's got class. You'll never hear a bad word from him or about him.

Bucky Dent

Dent was one of the biggest draws I ever had for a free autograph session. We had to cut the line off after 600 people, and Dent agreed to stay extra time to finish. Yankee fans love him: the photograph of his dramatic 1978 home run to win the pennant for the Yankees must have made up half the items he signed.

Bucky is a good card show guest, taking time to be friendly, converse and pose while maintaining a steady pace. He'll talk baseball, but prefers the short answer route. He's really a man of few words, although not afraid to speak his mind when he thinks he's being abused in public by hounds.

In public Bucky usually signs one-per-person, and limits the personalizations, photographs, and conversation. His penmanship is consistently sloppy, but that's his autograph. Mail produces limited, sporadic, and usually long-turnaround results. Bucky moves quickly, so you've got to stay alert to catch him.

Dent isn't one for the limelight, almost seeming to prefer going unnoticed. His behavior with autograph seekers is much like his playing days: he does the job, but in a quiet, no-frills manner. One positive vibe is that Bucky always seems to thank those who remind him of his big home run. He should, as that hit propelled him into a lifetime of fame.

Dwight "Doc" Gooden

Having hosted Gooden twice in his younger days and followed his career closely since, Gooden has been two different people, but is still a shy, introvert at heart. In younger days Gooden was the young radical, and success and riches brought him trouble.

Maturity and second chances made Gooden into the family man he is today. Hosting Dwight after his rookie season was quite a thrill. Talking with him then, it was almost as though he had just lived a dream and he wanted to find out if it was all true. By 1986, Gooden had experienced trouble with the law and drugs, and his image was tarnished. He rebounded, and after returning as what might be considered just an ordinary pitcher, he now lives a much quieter lifestyle. My guess is that like any other teenager, he just had to sow his wild oats.

Dwight is accommodating, although his shy nature won't provide much conversation. He stops for crowds and has a liking for kids. His signature hasn't changed much, and is still the sloppy scribble it has always been. Mail will go unanswered.

In public appearances, Dwight will again be quiet and reserved. He's glad to sign and will quickly move on to the next request. If you're looking for "Dr. K" to be loud and boisterous, you'll be disappointed. Modesty and shyness are the two main components of his personality.

Steve Garvey

Garvey handles himself well in all appearances, public and private. He's a willing signer, although he'll usually limit to one each in crowded situations. He exchanges conversation easily, although he's not the war story type.

He'll pose, personalize and take his time with each item. The signature becomes sloppier as the signing progresses. Sometimes you get the impression that Garvey is forcing the conversation, but mostly it's his way of making people feel welcome. Put a television camera in front of Steve and he gets even friendlier.

Garvey isn't much of a clown, but does possess a dry sense of humor. He always dresses well, keeping the image intact. Steve will voice displeasure on occasion with hounds who hand him many items at one time, often limiting them and refusing if he's sure he's already signed for that person. Even then, he doesn't raise his voice—he just states the facts.

Although it's difficult to tell if Garvey's friendliness is natural or forced, you still have to give him credit. This is his usual public behavior, and the majority of the time it leaves a positive impression.

Ferguson Jenkins

Jenkins is a quiet and shy man. He's a willing signer who will pose, personalize and converse, although he'll provide short answers. He almost acts bored with the signings, but that's his nature. He just doesn't seem excitable, although he's friendly and kind.

Jenkins will sign in public, but again, conversation will be limited. His shyness will take over. He's not going to tell you war stories. In crowds, Jenkins takes the time to sign, almost acting like it's easier than running away. Mail answers are few, so don't count on that method. His signature becomes sloppier as he goes along, but is still legible.

Fergie seems the kind who values his privacy and just goes about being an ordinary Joe. He's not going to be flashy, loud, or rude—instead, he's a slow and steady guy.

Juan Marichal

In most minds, the image of Marichal is a tough character with a short fuse. The clubbing of John Roseboro and images of this feisty competitor raising his voice to opponents leads you to believe that Juan is a hothead.

Nothing could be further from the truth; this is one friendly, accommodating and courteous person. He'll engage in conversation and tell stories, although they're usually short and to the point. He'll gladly personalize and pose for photos. This goes for both public and paid appearances. You'll hardly ever hear him raise his voice.

Marichal lives in the Dominican Republic, so forget about the mail route. He has beautiful penmanship that often looks as though it could be a fancy signature by a female. He is really a talkative sort of person who acts like one of the guys. Conversation comes easy for him.

Ask him about the Roseboro incident and he'll say it was something he'll always regret. Caught up in the heat of a pennant race, Marichal clubbed the Dodger catcher when he felt the catcher came too close to Juan's head while throwing the ball back to the pitcher.

Forget the image. This is a genuine good guy who simply lost his cool on the field of battle for just a moment. He is clearly a case of two different people, on and off the field: fiery competitor, nice guy.

Johnny Mize

A Southern gentleman is the best description I can give of Mize. Although he suffered many health problems in his later years, you never heard him complain. He went about his business in his usual kind and courteous style.

Mize didn't say much, believing in the "speak when you're spoken to" adage, He certainly wasn't a storyteller. When you saw him you saw his best behavior. Johnny would give whatever you wanted, and even returned his mail until his death.

Mize always had kind words and spoke highly of others. Rarely would you hear a negative word from him or about him. He might have been called the "Big Cat," but he was truly a lovable teddy bear.

Joe Morgan

The Morgan you hear doing baseball broadcasts is the real Joe Morgan. His broadcast style reveals much of his real personality. There's no fake here.

Joe is a great show guest. He personalizes, poses, willingly converses and is glad to share his baseball knowledge and stories. In public, much will depend on the circumstances. If it's a large and demanding crowd, expect Joe to limit access and look to escape. A small crowd will bring out his best.

I had pictured Joe as a tough cookie, primarily because his serious on-the-field focus leads you to believe he's all business. He's always more serious than fun and has a tendency to lay back and observe rather than jump in, so you'll see a quiet Joe most of the time. A great student of the game, he'll talk baseball anytime.

Morgan does possess one of the worst but most consistent signatures in sports. He realizes his duty to sign and moves fast, caring little for penmanship. Forget the mail, though; Joe's not going to return it.

For a little guy, Joe can make a big positive impression—just like his days on the playing field.

Ron LeFlore

Ron LeFlore's autobiography is titled *One In A Million*. It's the story of a convict that goes on to play major league baseball. It's hard to envision the LeFlore I know ever going to jail, he's really quite a character.

Ron is fun-loving, easy going, and a regular cutup. He's a willing signer, going to great efforts to please. He does like to get paid for it, though, often seeking appearances for such endeavors. He's cordial and always smiling. Whatever the customer wants, Ron will give him. He'll converse, provide stories, and revels in being one of the boys.

Since he's been out of baseball Ron has tried many different jobs and opportunities and seems to just be bouncing around. To his credit, he does keep going forward.

LeFlore is a fun guy to be around and would make a great minor league coach, as youngsters would have a hard time getting down around him. With his personality and life's experiences, he relates well to everybody.

Eddie Mathews

Although Eddie is a fun-loving and cooperative man, he's been plagued with a lifetime of drinking and smoking that have given him some serious health concerns. He has one of the sloppiest signatures in sports and in long sessions you'll have to be told whose autograph it is, since it becomes illegible.

Eddie can tell stories with the best of them. In sessions, he's great with the public and still manages to keep a quick steady pace. In public, Eddie is a signer, but you'll get a less friendly and cooperative attitude. Sometimes he can give you the impression you're bothering him. If he feels you're overstepping your bounds, he's not afraid to let you know.

Most of the time though Eddie will fit in as one of the guys, laughing and having fun. You have to really try hard to make him mad, and you won't see him that way very often. He does like his booze and smokes.

Fred McGriff

Since McGriff and I are both Tampa residents, there's more opportunity to keep up with the former Blue Jays, Padres, and Braves slugger. McGriff has got a good character but hates the entire autograph atmosphere. Hounds annoy him.

Fred is typical of today's well-known, long-time athletes in that he has no trouble refusing requests, despises hounds, and is disinterested in paid appearances. He'll sign, but almost out of necessity. Forget the mail and ballpark; he's going to avoid signing and when he does, it won't be for many.

In his two paid appearances with me, he clearly showed that he'd rather be elsewhere. His goal almost seemed to be to get done and move on. His personality is on the quiet side, but his demeanor speaks for him. In public, there's a strict limit of one. Sometimes, he'll just refuse to sign certain items. Fred's not going to win you with friendliness and kindness; that's not his nature. He may seem to be a good guy with a big smile when you see him, but let him confront a pack of autograph hounds and you'll see a guy who either grins and bears it or just refuses to sign—most likely the latter. Kids will get preference, however, in such situations.

Phil Rizzuto

"The Scooter" is a class act. He almost cracked my Top Ten Good Guys. He's personable, accommodating, unconcerned about time during appearances, and will gladly personalize and pose for photographs.

He is friendly, modest, and willing to carry on conversations. He won't tell long stories, but does enjoy talking about his Yankee playing days. He can make strangers feel like he's their lifelong friend.

You'll rarely hear Rizzuto raise his voice, lose his cool, or even use rough language. Even in crowded situations when Phil limits to one item each, he'll patiently take his time to satisfy all. He just seems to operate at a slower pace of life. On a team of rowdy Yankees, it's easy to see that Rizzuto was a steady, calming influence. He still has such qualities.

In an appearance at the Ted Williams Museum a few years back and the year after this Hall of Fame election, I heard Rizzuto say to donate the proceeds to the Museum (over $8,000) rather than be paid. Phil felt he owed Ted a favor after Williams went to bat for Phil's selection with the Old-Timer's Committee. He's got class—and his actions, words, and deeds show it.

Tony Perez

The first time I hosted Perez in 1986, it almost turned into a nightmare. That's when Maria Gutierrez bailed me out. Tony was having trouble spelling names in the English language when Maria sat with him and kept things in order. I believe that much of Perez's disposition comes from this trouble with the language, which interferes with his ability to communicate.

Tony is another who is two different people at appearances and in public. At appearances he is courteous and will pose for photos and personalize (although you have to often help with spelling), but he moves quickly and doesn't slow down for much. He'll converse, but expect short answers. He won't say much or provide you with stories and often won't speak unless spoken to. You'll know when he's mad, though, as he'll raise his voice and give you a cold stare.

In public, you could get an outright refusal or the most accommodating person in the world, depending on the circumstances. Most likely you'll get a quick signature and not much else. If you hand him six cards, he'll sign one and hand the other five back. Forget the mail route, as Tony won't return it. Tony was a great player, and was elected in the Hall of Fame in 2000. Since his personality reflects his lifestyle of quietly going about his business, there was much doubt over his chances. But now he's in. It will increase the demand drastically.

Duke Snider

Here's a classy good guy who one can see has fun at appearances. Whatever you want—personalization, conversation, stories, or photographs—Duke will give it to you. In public, Duke is good for one autograph and politely tells you that's his limit. His distinctive signature always looks the same and he takes his time to make sure of it. This fits in well with his signings, as he's in a slow, talking mood during these times.

In public Duke is much the same, except for limiting conversation and sticking to the signing at hand during crowded situations. He used to return mail requests with a request for payment to charity, even though it would take many months to respond. Duke has a positive outlook on things and you'll rarely hear negative or foul language. He's not one for nostalgia about the old days.

At the time of Duke's appearance, I had convinced my wife to purchase a satellite dish with profits from the show. After I lost big money on Snider, the dish went down the drain. (See Chapter Eight for complete details.) Duke might be a nice guy, but the public seemed disinterested in him. The hounds later told me he signs items in the mail for $5, and that my charge of $20 was too much.

Jackie Smith

I drove Smith crazy with all my talk of fantasy football. He'd grin and bear it, but almost seemed disinterested. Instead, he would dive into topics like family, business, and politics. He seems highly educated, and counters the dumb jock image with a strong vocabulary and interest in the opinions of others. Unlike many athletes, he doesn't seem to miss the game. He's moved on to other pursuits.

Smith is polite, accommodating, and almost seems bored with appearances. He moves at a brisk pace, but will do what's asked. He'll sign in public, but don't expect much more. He doesn't quite agree with the autograph craze, but is willing to make a few bucks from signing his name at the appearances.

Interestingly, Smith will sign photos and cards of his famous Super Bowl touchdown pass drop, although it's quite a bit sloppier than his usual signature. While it's obvious the drop is a sore subject, he doesn't dwell on it. He'll tell you that although the memory is still painful, he's learned to live with it. After almost 20 years, that drop is unfortunately the image many fans have of Smith. It's unfair, but that's life. He deserves better.

Ralph Kiner

Kiner's personality resembles that of Duke Snider. Considering the fact that both played at the same time, compiled similar statistics, and later became baseball broadcasters, it seems a natural progression.

Kiner will gladly personalize, converse, pose, and do what's requested. He won't say much, and is an observer more than a talker. Just like Duke, in crowds Ralph will tend to converse less in an effort to speed up the signing process. Kiner has a very consistent signature, and usually returns mail requests with one of his own for charity signings. He's not the speedy type, and exhibits a great deal of class in his speech. You'll rarely hear anything negative from Kiner.

Simply put, Ralph may be the master of the malaprop but he's got lots of class, and after all his years of fame still remains a solid, down to earth guy.

Bobby Thomson

Thomson became forever embedded in American sports lore with his 1951 pennant-winning homer for the New York Giants. Despite almost 50 years of constant reminders, his modesty remains. His attitude seems to indicate that he was just lucky enough to be at the right place at the right time.

Bobby is a soft-spoken man who seems to move in slow motion. He's never in a hurry, and takes his time to make sure he's given you what you requested. He poses, converses, and personalizes, moving even slower for those who paid for the autograph. He often places the date of that homer—October 3, 1951—with his signature, which is always neat, clean, and consistent.

Bobby returns mail, but there's often up to a six-month turnaround. He's a guy that has trouble saying "no" and is truly honored you asked. His actions indicate it's not a bother, and he almost seems amazed by all the attention.

Many times, fate turns jerks into heroes. In this case, fate couldn't have picked a nicer guy. He's worn it well for a long time and has never let it go to his head.

Buck Leonard

Unfortunately, I hosted Buck Leonard when he was 88 years old and in poor health, the result of a stroke that paralyzed him on one side, forcing him to write with his other hand. Buck was escorted by his wife and son, and the autograph session was a testament to his fortitude.

Leonard was a Hall of Famer who made his mark in the Negro Leagues but did not receive the honor until in his 80's. Thus he was a relative unknown until then. The effects of the stroke made appearances a hardship for Leonard but he did a few each year to supplement his income.

Buck agreed to sign 300 items in his appearance and did the first 200 in about three hours. The last 100 took almost two hours with frequent breaks to rest. To Leonard's credit, he would personalize and pose, but limited conversation in an effort to keep things moving. His wife seemed to have the ability to keep him going, but it was difficult to get to know the real Leonard.

The man I saw earned my respect. Despite the difficulty, he agreed to do as asked and took his time so that every signature looked the same—neat, clean and consistent. Soon after this, Buck discontinued his appearances and limited his signing to mail requests, where time and physical demands were less taxing.

Bill Mazeroski

"Maz" is one of my childhood heroes, so there was more anticipation in meeting the Pirate great. I found Mazeroski to be well worth the status of hero. He was kind, cooperative, and talkative, always taking the time to fulfill all requests, most of which asked him to add the date of his World Series winning homer (October 13, 1960) to his autograph.

In private Maz is much the same, but will limit the numbers and be less talkative in crowded situations. He's got an honesty that will give you a surprising answer—not the programmed standard one you might expect. If you ask him about the Hall of Fame, he'll tell you he thinks he deserves the honor, but he's not consumed with it.

Mazeroski will take his time to make each autograph a clean, neat signature. Mail results are unpredictable. In his playing days, you'd always see Maz with a big wad of chewing tobacco in his jaw. Today the chewing habit is gone and the body a bit rounder.

However, Mazeroski's hero status was forever secured one late afternoon in October, 1960 when he approached home plate holding his batting helmet in the air, apparently walking on clouds. He's honored that moment for almost 40 years with behavior and a personality befitting of a hero.

Lance Parrish

This is another athlete who received strong consideration for the Top Ten Good Guys list. Lance would never walk past a crowd of autograph seekers. He always has the time to stop, and gives a clean, quality signature at all times. He's the same in both private and public. He'll converse, be glad to pose, personalize, and often sign multiples in crowded situations.

Lance has one of the most consistent signatures in sports. It has a female flair about it, but is neat and clean. You'll never see him in a hurry. He always seems to have kind words and be in a good mood.

I've seen Lance stop and sign for crowds as large as 100 people near the locker room after games, while countless teammates walked by the appeals. He's maintained a modesty and true affection for the fans. Parrish strikes you as just one of the neighborhood fellows who realizes he got lucky. You'll never see him lose his cool. Maybe that's why he's never lost touch.

Sandy Koufax

Although I have never hosted Koufax in an appearance, I've had plenty of encounters with the former Dodger great. His fee is almost prohibitive; at last report $100,000 for 2,000 autographs.

Koufax used to hang out with the Dodgers in Vero Beach during spring training, and if you were patient he'd sign for you. He would avoid the larger crowds, staying out of sight only to resurface, often in street clothes, when the crowds lessened.

He'd be willing to pose, personalize, and converse once you got him, but most of the time it was a one item per person limit.

In the early 1990s, Koufax seemed to quit coming to Dodgertown. Since he does few shows and does not return mail, it's impossible to get Sandy as he just doesn't seem to surface much. When he does, he's unfailingly cordial, accommodating, and polite. At shows he steps up to an even higher level, giving the fans more conversation and feedback.

Seeing more of him is the problem.

Hal Newhouser

Hal was the feisty type. He could be extremely cooperative, or just plain refuse. His general policy in public was that he would sign, but it was not wise to ask him for more than one autograph. In paid appearances, he'd do whatever was asked.

Newhouser stayed consistent with his signature from start to finish and would rather be neat than fast, although he would limit conversation to keep things moving. Rather than long answers and stories, he gave short, to-the-point answers. Because he played from 1939–1955, it sometimes took him a while to come up with the answer, but he eventually would. Details took time to recall.

In his second appearance with me, Hal had hurt his back the day before. You could tell he was in obvious pain with every step. He told me, he thought "The fans and you are counting on me, and I didn't want to let them down." He put on his best face for the three hours, and though he needed help walking and getting in and out of vehicles, he never complained.

Needless to say, Hal was from the old school—raised to do what's expected, despite the obstacles. Only age and fame made him a bit of a crusty, old fart. He'd grumble, but usually do what was asked. He passed away in 1999.

Mel Allen

Allen was a guest for me when he was in his early 80s, but the voice was still distinctively Allen; hearing it was like hearing a piece of Americana. Allen was a kind, gracious man who always took his time and made you glad you came.

During his appearance he rambled on with long stories, often forgetting or correcting names, but you loved him because you knew he was trying. He signed items with some of his customary phrases, including his trademark, "How 'Bout That?" He welcomed photos and personalizations, all the while

Mel Allen with the family— "Mr. How 'Bout That?" just kept talking and talking, but you loved the stories.—Photo by Joanne Thresher

taking his time and providing every person with a clean, neat, consistent signature.

In public, Mel was much the same. It's clear that he felt blessed in life and enjoyed the moment. You never heard Allen speak negatively of another, or use rough language. He was just easy, slow going. No hurry here.

In today's era of hip, slang-filled screaming broadcasters, it's doubtful that Mel would fit in. "Smooth" is the best word to describe Allen and his style. It's tough to find such broadcasters today. They just don't measure up to "Going, going . . . gone!"

Ralph Houk

Houk enjoys retired life in Winter Haven, Florida, and now devotes more time to golf and family travels than baseball. He's done a number of appearances for me, and every time has been a gentleman.

He'll do whatever is asked of him, although in public one should expect less conversation and more limits on the numbers. The mail route produces mixed results, but more than one request in the letter is usually ignored.

Ralph won't badmouth the game and other players although he'll tell you that money has changed the game—and not necessarily for the better. Houk believes money has created the pampered, spoiled athlete common today, but by the same principle he'll also tell you, "They'd be nuts to pass up the money being tossed around today."

Houk is a polite, low-key, down-to-earth guy. You can tell he doesn't miss baseball. It provided him with a good life, but golf has taken its place.

Tony Gwynn

Gwynn is a funny guy who enjoys life. In appearances he will accommodate any request, including photos, personalizations, and conversation. He's not a storyteller but loves humorous incidents. He has the ability to leave you laughing. His smile is constant.

The quality of Tony's signature is one of the most consistent in sports. He always provides a clean, neat autograph. In public, he's become tougher through the years, but will, generally, still fulfill requests. However, don't expect multiple numbers.

During his appearance, Gwynn talked about the fantasy sports players. One year, when he was doing badly at the start, the fantasy players criticized him and he said they had "wasted their money." After going on a tear in the second half to win the batting title, Gwynn said laughingly to those same people, "Great job. I'm glad I picked you."

Tony likes to have fun, often seeing the humor in everyday life. I think that's part of the reason for his success; along with a great work ethic, he's been able to laugh and place things in perspective.

Gwynn was, unfortunately, one of my most disappointing draws, as are most black singles hitters. As a person, he left a positive impression on all who came, acting like he was just one of the boys and not anybody special. He's a fun guy to be around.

Phil Niekro

Niekro is a quiet, friendly man who has changed much since his induction into the Hall of Fame. At appearances he's Mr. Nice Guy, taking his time and meeting all special requests. He's not going to say much, and short answers are the rule. In public, he'll avoid the crowd and place limitations on the numbers. Although he won't raise his voice, he'll let you know when you've crossed the line.

In appearances he takes his time, providing a neat clean autograph. He's not a storyteller, but enjoys small talk. He smiles and seems to enjoy himself. The public Niekro is great at golf and charitable appearances, but a bit more distant at other functions. He'll often grin and bear it. Before his Hall of Fame status, he rarely refused. Now, it happens much more frequently. Forget the mail—he's not going to answer it. With his election obviously he realized that there's more to be made from appearances, although his fee is considered too high for his drawing ability.

It's my belief the hounds have toughened his skin, although he can still be a good guy when he wants to be.

Goose Gossage

One would think that because of the memory of Gossage standing on the mound with his intimidating glare on a mean face that this is one tough cookie. Don't be fooled—it's all part of the act.

As it turns out, the Goose is actually a friendly, soft-spoken individual who sometimes seems awkward in conversation, so he says little. He'll gladly pose, personalize, and honor other requests. After you thank him, he often thanks you back or says, "You're welcome." That's quite a difference from what one would expect, based on that pitcher's mound image.

The Goose has poor penmanship, but still takes his time to give you his best. He's not in a hurry, but rather enjoys the feedback. Goose won't woo you with stories, but he loves to laugh. In public Gossage is much the same, but he moves faster and it's almost as though you have to trap the Goose. In large crowds he'll sign for all, limiting individual numbers and moving more quickly.

Now that he's retired, it's safe for batters to know that the mound presence was all part of the act, and that the Goose is a nice guy. Maybe that image helped his fastball.

Frank "Tug" McGraw

If there was ever a case of a guy saying exactly what's on his mind, it is Frank "Tug" McGraw. Expect the unexpected with Tug.

He might chastise you for bothering him for an autograph—or invite you to pose with him. He could act like he's irate with your request, then after a two-minute tirade say, "Sure, I'll be glad to do that." Tug loves to be the center of attention and has fun in all situations.

In appearances, Tug goes with the flow. He can joke, clown, be serious, get mad, start singing, or get up and take a break. When the spirit moves McGraw he's going to follow it, but most of the time Tug will be a friendly, accommodating gentleman who loves to joke with the ladies. Tug will always provide a clean, neat signature, punctuated with his trademark smiling face. The mail route will provide little luck.

In public, McGraw is not as free a signer. He seems to take pride in turning down or toying with the hounds. He'll often joke with them about how much the item is now worth. McGraw seems to have a good time in all he does, but enjoys ruffling feathers along the way. You just have to realize that most of the time he's just having fun.

Since son Tim McGraw is now a country music superstar, don't be surprised if Tug wails out some of the tunes. You just never know what he's going to do next. The man is as off-the-wall as they come, and always seems to be turning things into a good time.

Frank Robinson

Frank is clearly a member of the chip-on-the-shoulder brigade of black players of the 50s. At one time a free autograph was impossible, although he's loosened up just slightly since he began working for the commissioner's office. In the past he would possibly sign one in 50 requests; now it's one in 25. Most of the time it's a stern "no" or a shake of the head. Don't waste time on the mail route—it's not coming back.

At paid appearances, Frank will be cordial, accommodating, and willing to do what's requested, including personalizations and photos. He often displays a sense of humor bordering on sarcasm. One might ask him to sign a photo for Bobby, and Frank might throw back a comment like, "I'll do this, but Bobby doesn't deserve it. He's been a bad boy." He doesn't mean any harm by most comments, and is just having fun.

Frank will gladly converse, although he won't go into long stories or revive old incidents. Instead, he'll give you short, candid answers. You can tell he's not crazy about the entire autograph scene, except when he's getting paid for signing. That compensation assures you a clean, neat signature. It's a longshot for a freebie, although the chances increase if you are a beautiful woman. It's evident Frank likes such creatures, often picking them out of the crowd.

Kirby Puckett

Kirby is one of the athletes who worked through all five stages referred to in chapter three. He started as a most accommodating individual, but by the time he retired he would refuse more than sign. He doesn't do appearances, since he can't bear the thought of having a fee attached to his name.

If you do get Puckett, expect a fast, almost illegible autograph. You had better hope the crowd is small, and even at that it's still one each. He doesn't like personalizations, and will pose for photos only if you're ready and all he has to do is look up. Kirby's going to avoid the crowd if possible and most of the time will just outright refuse, often providing some type of excuse.

When you do pin Kirby down he'll converse, but expect short, quick answers. Over the years, it's become evident that Puckett has come to despise the autograph industry and that after seeing many of the same hounds, he's simply learned to refuse. Children stand a greater chance, as Kirby will pick them out first—but again, it's got to be the luck of the right place at the right time.

Pee Wee Reese

Reese made probably one paid appearance per year, that being one for a New York promoter that he had befriended over the years. In public Reese was a cordial, accommodating signer. In appearances, he was even better.

The best places to get Reese were the golf course and charitable functions. He'd even sign multiple items if time permitted and the crowd was small. Sometimes, he'd sign more than one just to avoid a scene. He was willing to personalize, pose and converse. He'd handle your item with care and give it a clean, neat signature. This was a true gentleman.

Reese was the quiet, laid-back type. He'd wait his turn to speak, didn't say much, and seldom said anything critical of another. Even in crowded, pushy situations, he maintained his composure. The mail route produced mixed results that depended on Pee Wee's health, which worsened in the past few years. Over the years, the mail became less productive. He passed away in 1999.

It's obvious that Reese didn't like large crowds, clearly displaying paranoia about such situations. Most speculate that's why he limited public appearances, preferring his local Florida golf course rather than using his celebrity to play at larger, better known courses. He'd rather have stayed out of the limelight after his day in the sun.

Jim Palmer

Palmer is a most accommodating and friendly signer, and received serious consideration for my Top Ten Good Guys. In appearances, he's perfect in that he does all that's requested while still signing at a quick pace.

In public, Jim is much the same, and will often chide those who ask for multiple signatures. His comments in those circumstances range from "How do I know you're not going to sell this one?" to "Make sure your brother gets that one." Often he just rolls with the punches, knowing the hounds will beat him out of a few autographs and potentially, a few dollars.

The quality of Jim Palmer's signatures leaves much to be desired. Often, you must be told who it is to make it out. By the end of the appearance, it begins to get even worse. Mail is a hit-and-mostly-miss situation, and over the years the chances of getting a return have become less and less likely.

Palmer fits in like

Jim Palmer with Sue. This made her day. Jim's a super nice guy, and says he doesn't dye his hair.
—Photo by Joanne Thresher

one of the boys. He likes to tell stories, usually with twisted or funny endings. He plays the role for the female set, speaking kindly and inviting personalizations and photos. Jim adapts well, often breaking the ice with shy fans. He can be serious, but more often than not he's clowning or telling some tongue-in-cheek story.

Ask him about Earl Weaver, his longtime manager and adversary, and Jim tells you much of that was overblown. They didn't always agree, but Palmer respected Weaver and at times, just liked to get Earl's goat. Jim still maintains a big ego and is not afraid to talk about himself.

Most interestingly, Palmer still maintains his youthful appearance and dark hair with no hint of gray. Ask him whether he dyes it and he'll say he doesn't. Tough to believe, but remember—this is a guy who can cut up and instigate with a perfectly straight face. Even so, he's very likable.

Stan Musial

Mostly a gentleman, but occasionally he will lose his cool and refuse requests, especially when he thinks the hounds are abusing him. At appearances Musial is a most accommodating signer, agreeing to personalizations, photographs and gladly exchanging small talk. He's made many friends through the years and seems to know tons of people.

Stan won't tell long elaborate stories, but he has good recall of his events and incidents. His penmanship needs some work and gets sloppier as he goes. In the higher number signings such autographs are sometimes illegible, especially when signing on small items.

In public, Stan doesn't mind signing, but gets annoyed in crowded situations when he's asked for multiples and will sometimes just stop signing. Mail is usually not returned.

Musial will rarely speak negatively or critically of another and is really a man of few words. At appearances he might stop and play a tune on his harmonica, often, "Take Me Out to the Ballgame." He likes to have fun and has learned to live with the hounds, but you can tell he despises pushy, demanding signature seekers.

His nickname may be "Stan the Man," but mostly he is "Stan the Gentleman."

Tommy Lasorda

Although generally accommodating, Lasorda becomes a prince when the TV camera is on him. He has a deep affection for kids and ladies, often approaching them first in crowds.

Tommy limits appearances to perhaps one per year, due to a combination of disliking and disbelieving in them. At an appearance you get a friendly, lovable character who goes out of his way to satisfy the crowd. Photos, personalization, and conversation are permissible. In fact, talking often causes Lasorda to forget his task and things slow to a crawl. He's got more war stories than the American history books and he can put a great spin on each one.

In public, Tommy becomes tougher. Forget a second signature—Lasorda will let you know if you've received one already and sternly refuse. Tommy can go as the situation dictates: "Mr. Nice Guy," or "Mr. No." Tommy will often sign for a few minutes, then bolt, saying he must go. He likes to be the life of the party and fits in great with the guys. Lasorda will converse on any subject, always making sure he's offered his opinion.

Since his election into the Hall of Fame Tommy has become less accommodating, seeming to sense that the hounds are taking advantage of his casual nature. He can offer some rough language when angry or protective of his turf. Once upon a time, he signed for everyone. Now he accommodates most requests unless he is feeling overwhelmed, at which time he'll find an excuse; or abused, in which case he'll flatly refuse. Get a TV camera and it's a guarantee. He'll sign for all.

Bob Lemon

Lemon didn't have much of a personality. He was quiet and said little. To his credit, he was willing to do what was asked in appearances, including photos, personalizations and talk, although you'd have to carry the conversation and received short answers, not war stories.

In public, he'd sign, preferring the grin and bear it route. He wasn't going to win you over with kindness. He'd just do what was asked. To his credit, he rarely refused to sign. The signature stayed the same, and like Yogi Berra, remained the same size, regardless of the size of the item to be signed.

Lemon seemed to live in the middle. You never saw him get angry or overly excited. It's accepted that he lived a tough life, with cigarettes and alcohol being a large part of his routine. However, he wouldn't bad-mouth or criticize others, or make you believe the old days were better.

In one of our discussions he gave me his opinion of George Steinbrenner, who fired him when Lemon was manager of the Yankees—despite the fact that he led the team to the World Championship in 1978. "There's nothing wrong with George; he just wants to win," Lemon told me.

Bob understood the autograph game. Just sign: you don't have to win a personality contest. He never did, but that was his style.

Chuck Bednarik

A member of the old school who comes off as one of the boys in appearances. He'll do whatever is asked including photos, personalizations, and taking time to talk. Chuck has a ton of war stories and tells them well, often jazzing them up to make them colorful and funny. He loves to be the life of the party and takes his time to make each signature a neat, clean one, without time being a factor.

In public much depends on his mood, but most likely Bednarik will take the time to offer his signature. In crowds, he'll politely limit the numbers for each person. He'll accommodate all special requests, but keeps things moving by making less talk and more action. He's loud, and has opinions about everything.

What amazed me about Bednarik was his physical condition. Many of his fingers are twisted, and his nose shows a sideward tilt. It's obvious the game of football meant much to him in enduring such injuries. This "old school veteran" often took a beating, almost wearing those lifetime wounds as a badge of honor.

An interesting observation about Bednarik was his attitudes about racial issues and black athletes. He felt that black athletes did not appreciate their sport, mostly because of their dancing, showboating, and prima donna attitudes. He claimed that in his playing days such attitudes would have encouraged others to "take matters into their own hands." Again, many of the old school grew up with those attitudes and some never lost them. The question is, was such talk real or just an act to fit in with the boys? I hope that it is the former.

Roosevelt Brown

Another member of the old school with the scars to prove it. Brown, a quiet, soft-spoken man, has a crippled knee that slows him and makes it difficult to sit for long periods and get in and out of automobiles. The New York Giant Hall of Fame tackle doesn't complain, just goes about his business as if the injury was just one of the prices he paid to play.

In appearances, this is a guy much like his personality—a slow, steady, polite, and unassuming individual. He'll gladly fulfill special requests, and take his time to make sure you got a clean, quality signature every time. He'll converse, but says little and offers short answers. Brown is surely not a storyteller.

In public, Brown is much the same. He signs, rarely refusing requests, but again expect a signature and not much conversation and exchange. It's just his nature. Sometimes, even Brown has trouble with his memory, often spending long periods trying to recall a name, place, or date.

It's guys like Brown that seem to have been forgotten. Their playing days and glory long concluded and replaced by today's heroes, former greats like Brown seem to enjoy the appearance route. It's not only a chance to make a few bucks, but also allows the athlete to again be a hero for that short period. Such signers want to do well. Most of the time, as in the case of Brown, they do.

Raymond Berry

A gentleman. After you've spent a few hours with Berry it's hard to perceive him as a Hall of Fame football player. He just doesn't seem tough enough. Perhaps his limited success as a coach can be attributed to the nice guy role. You just couldn't see him exploding at a player.

I've never seen Berry angry. He goes out of his way to please. Whatever you want Raymond will deliver either in public or appearances. Photos, greetings, or small talk are no problem to the former Colt.

Berry is quiet, but will engage in conversation if you lead the way. He's got a great memory for facts, places, and dates. You just won't hear abusive language or anything negative. He's just a laid-back guy.

Raymond was a disappointing draw for me, considering his legendary status. Those who came saw a polite, considerate, and well dressed man. Berry carries himself well.

Old number 82 is a winner, on and off the field.

Trent Dilfer

Hosting Dilfer at the conclusion of his rookie season, I found the quarterback to be personable and extremely confident. Although he had played little and the jury was still out on his abilities, Dilfer seemed to possess a cocksure attitude.

During his appearance, Dilfer seemed to be enjoying himself in the first hour, usually engaging in conversation, writing extra when asked, and agreeing to photos. In the second hour, Dilfer obviously enjoyed himself less, and began watching the clock for the end of his two hour session.

Dilfer has changed much over the years, often refusing autographs, doing fewer appearances, and preferring children over adults. He's always had a sloppy signature, but over the years it has gotten worse. He's also maintained the habit of placing a Bible scripture after his name.

Dilfer will confer, but offers only short answers. He's been lambasted in the Tampa media for failure to live up to his high draft status, and at times, it seems like he's trying to stay out of the limelight.

In some ways that failure exemplifies what is wrong with the NFL. The high draft picks are paid highly for potential and when they don't live up to expectations, they still walk away with the cash. Usually in our society, you perform and are then rewarded. That's not always so in sports.

Dilfer seemed to enjoy the adulation in those early days. Only time will prove whether it was well-founded or not.

Joe Greene

One of my personal favorites because of my Steeler allegiance. Interestingly, Joe told me that he has never signed his name "Mean" Joe Greene. When I told him I knew people who said they'd obtained that with their autograph from him, he told me tersely, "Well they're lying. That's not my name."

Joe is one of the "let's get this over with," crew—although, to his credit, he does all that's asked. He'll gladly pose for pictures, personalize and engage in conversation. He has a laid-back approach to the process that, at times, seems almost like boredom.

In public, Joe's a great signer, but will usually limit the numbers per person. In one of my requests at a Super Bowl XXV gathering in Tampa, Joe said, "Man, I must have signed everything in Florida by now."

Joe won't say much. He'll provide short answers and has a dry wit that sometimes borders on sarcasm. It's his way of joking. He's easygoing, but when provoked he'll tell you where you stand. His tone of voice will change and you'll know you've gone too far. He might then refuse to sign, or just say nothing and sign anyway.

"Mean" Joe Greene. As a Steeler fan, he was one of my favorite guests. He says he doesn't sign the name "Mean" Joe Greene, even with the huge hands.—Photo by Joanne Thresher

One sidelight: Greene has huge, strong hands. It's easy to see how he manhandled offensive linemen. But for hounds he grins and bears it, realizing it's easier to cooperate than fight the crowd.

Dick Butkus

One of the toughest players ever in football history, Butkus is one nice guy off the field most of the time. He can get testy when pressed for what he considers our "unreasonable" demands. He doesn't hide his emotions well, so you'll know when he's not in a pleasant mood. This usually means snappy answers in an obviously angry tone.

When hosting Butkus in an autograph session, one is wise to limit it to two hours. He gets antsy after that. When he is with the public though, he'll meet all requests for photos and personalizations. He's glad to engage in conversation and his recall

Dick Butkus with Matt and Andrew. Dick got testy after two hours, but his count showed incredible concentration.—Photo by Joanne Thresher

is amazing. He wants to make very sure the attendee gets their money's worth. His signature will stay consistent throughout the signing.

Dick will usually sign in public, but limits the numbers. He'll keep things moving in crowds so we can finish quickly and move on. There's probably less chatter and a more deliberate attempt to finish. Again, Dick is quick to snap back if he feels he's being abused.

Butkus walks with a limp and many of his fingers are permanently twisted: the rewards of hard play in his sport. Inquiries into these battle scars lead you to believe he regards them as part of the game with little complaint.

Perhaps what amazed me most about the "Bear great" was that he kept count of how many signatures he had signed during his session without anyone else knowing. He had a counter on his foot. We did 635, and he came within five of that number. It was hard to imagine such concentration among all the chaos surrounding him for three hours. Overall, old #51 represents Chicago and himself well, although he can be feisty at times.

Sam Huff

Another case of a rough, tough guy being classy and cooperative. Huff signs willingly in public, always going the extra mile if asked. In autograph sessions, he's even more of a prince.

Sam will personalize, pose and converse, often getting into such prolonged conversations that he must be reminded there are others waiting. He'll offer an opinion on any subject from politics to sports, and will listen to your offerings. He's polite, courteous, and well-spoken.

Now a Redskins broadcaster, Huff seems to like the adulation and recognition. Unlike many athletes, he won't shy away from the crowd and he handles it well.

I don't think you'll hear a bad word about Sam Huff. It's tough to find one.

Gino Marchetti

Don Shula called him "the best defensive player I ever coached." Gino was an animal on the field, and is a nice guy off. He's most cooperative, and you'll rarely see him refuse an autograph request.

He'll pose, personalize, and converse, although you have to lead the conversation. Marchetti seems to have a shyness that dictates short answers. Sometimes he gets dates and places mixed up, but it's not intentional. He's not fond of talking about himself.

Gino's not in a hurry and seems always to move at a slow pace, due in part to the many injuries that have lingered through the years. His aim while signing is to please the public. He'll do what's asked.

Marchetti also has a dry wit. Some of his answers will come out funny, although he isn't trying to be a comedian. When asked "Who was the toughest guy you ever played against," he chimed out, "Too many of them."

The Colt great is quality, off and on the field.

Lenny Moore

This former Colt great can talk up a storm on any subject. Lenny is a cooperative, pleasant and easygoing man. He'll do what's asked in public or at autograph sessions. Be careful with conversation because once you get him going, you can't stop him. Furthermore, a remarkable memory allows Lenny to fill in all the blanks.

He has an intelligence that shows in his speech, vocabulary and knowledge.

Interestingly, Lenny and I somehow got into a conversation about the black athlete of the 1950s. At that time, integration was just starting. We spoke much about the hardships and abuse that black athletes of that era experienced. Moore relayed that there is still some hurt because of those days; racial taunts and injustice left lifetime scars.

Moore told me that while the situation has greatly improved in the last 50 years, little credit is given to the pioneers of that period. When I mentioned he ought to write a book about those days, Moore said he had been giving it much thought. If he writes as well as he talks, it will be an interesting (and long) book.

Hardy Nickerson

Hardy owns god-like status in the Tampa area. On and off the field he's been all quality. Nickerson came to the Bucs in 1993 after six seasons with the Steelers, where his hard-nosed play built a reputation. Through the years, Hardy has matured from the quiet, soft-spoken athlete to a community leader involved in many causes and charities.

For three years Hardy refused to do appearances, because he didn't want to charge for his autograph. In 1995 he finally agreed to appear, as long as the charge didn't exceed $5. I still believe he felt uncomfortable with any fee and has therefore done only a few appearances since then, and none when there's been a charge.

In appearances, Hardy is a gem. He'll sign, personalize and pose for photos. Nickerson will converse, but his shyness provides smaller answers. You'll have to carry the conversation.

In public, Nickerson will sometimes refuse when crowds are large, although the vast majority of the time he'll sign. In larger groups his mind is on signing, so he'll limit conversation and stick to the task. He's well-spoken when required to speak. On the field Hardy can sometimes display wild emotions, such as doing body poses, pointing, and talking trash. After 10 minutes with him off the field, you'd never believe him capable of such actions. There's a modesty and humility about this man. Maybe that's why the fans love him. He's now playing in Jacksonville.

Dick "Night Train" Lane

Dick is one of those guys who will keep you laughing. He's funny, even when he doesn't try to be. He's definitely old school, but gives credit to today's players. He told me he thought today's athletes were better physically, better trained and coached, but maybe not as tough as those in his day.

Although he's had many health problems in the last few years that have slowed him down, "Night Train" is cordial, cooperative, and aims to please. He takes his time with each signature so that they all look the same—always clean and neat. Photos are no problem. He has the same attitude at appearances or in public. I think he just wants to be remembered.

An example of Lane's humor was displayed at his public session with me. When handed a football with many signatures on it, Lane asked the owner, "Where do you want me to sign it?" "Anywhere you can fit it," the owner replied. After observing the ball and seeing there were few available spaces, Lane said, "Ah, heck, we're all professionals at this. Let's just put it here." Lane then proceeded to neatly sign the ball and hand it back.

For a guy that was famous for the clothesline tackle, Lane certainly was nice off the field. A real professional, and a naturally funny man.

Johnny Unitas

Unitas was one of my most disappointing draws. In 1990, I sold only 350 tickets for his appearance, despite the bargain rate of $8 per any item. With his legendary status, I expected more.

I found Unitas to be personable, cooperative and willing to personalize and allow photographs, and with a personality that could speak on any subject. He had a high opinion of himself and was sometimes joking, but mostly serious. When I asked him who he considered the greatest quarterback ever, he replied, "Me. A quarterback has to feel that way."

Over the years, Unitas has done fewer appearances because he has set a much higher fee.

In public, he has toughened his stance. He used to be a willing and carefree signer, but has placed limits and even occasionally refused. When he does appear, Unitas will gladly answer questions and special requests. He moves slowly in order to give those in attendance his best. The signature maintains its consistency and almost seems to have a backward slant.

Johnny U. will offer his opinion on any subject, and you'll hear a lot of old school in his answers. He's another who thinks the game was tougher in his era. When you take a close look at him you'll see the bent fingers and nose, the battle scars of his career.

He may have a big ego, but he still acts like one of the boys when he's in the crowd.

Y.A. Tittle

One of the classiest guys I have ever met, and truly a gentleman. He is polite, courteous, cooperative and friendly in public and at appearances. He doesn't worry about time and takes his time with each person and signature. He simply reminds you to let him know when he's finished. He engages requests with detailed conversations filled with incredible recall of persons, places and things.

If you have a unique older piece, you can expect Tittle to ask about it. He'll examine it with a careful eye and inquiring about its origin or history. Tittle did not save memorabilia before the 1980s like many other athletes . . . so he relishes those second chances to view them.

Tittle's not of the old school. He has praise for all, saying that he feels a good athlete would excel no matter what the circumstances. You'll never hear a foul word or criticism of others. He's got too much class.

Doug Williams

First, let it be said that Williams is a hero in Tampa. Previous to the last few seasons, he was the only quarterback to lead the Buccaneers to three playoff appearances from 1979–1982. Then he left in a contract dispute, going on to become a Super Bowl Most Valuable Player with the Washington Redskins.

Williams is cooperative and pleasant in appearances, although in public he's a bit tougher and usually limits the numbers and declines personalizations. You'll have to carry on the conversations—although if you hit the right topic, such as the Buccaneers or racial relations, you can set him off. Photographs are no problem, but at times you can see he's just grinning and bearing it. His signature can be sloppy at times, so smart promoters won't rush him and will instead go with his pace.

For a long time, Doug had hard feelings about his final days in Tampa, but seems to have mellowed over the years. The Super Bowl ring and MVP award have eased the pain some, but there's still some bitterness. Hopefully, time will heal all wounds.

Bart Starr

Although I've never hosted Starr in an appearance, I've had encounters with him twice. These were at a charity tennis tournament and a fund-raising banquet. He's polite, cooperative, friendly, and a willing signer. Special requests and photographs are no problem.

Starr doesn't like appearances, often turning them down or setting a high fee. But even in public, he'll take his time, providing neat autographs for all. When you look at his failure as a coach, you'd almost attribute it to being too friendly. He doesn't seem to have a mean bone in his body, and even in crowded, demanding situations, he maintains his cool.

The two-time Super Bowl MVP speaks little, and you'll have to lead the conversation. You won't hear criticism, foul language or cries that the old school was better. This is one cool customer, just like his Packer quarterback days.

Terry Bradshaw

The Terry Bradshaw you see cutting up and having fun on the network studio shows is the real one. This is a guy who appears to have fun all the time.

But in public Bradshaw is a bit different, often turning down requests. He'll sign more often that not, but will do so hurriedly and with little fanfare. If you want a personalization or photograph, the smaller the crowd the greater your chances. It's said that his wife (now his ex) and his secretary signed much of his mail, but he won't confirm or deny that rumor.

In appearances he moves slowly, often exchanging conversation and getting into long discussions. You have to remind him to keep moving. His signature starts sloppy and gets worse. He will personalize and pose for photographs. Speed isn't on his mind. It's the satisfaction of those who are obtaining the signature. He's got a lot of the old school in him, but you won't hear much criticism of athletes. Coaches are a target, however, as his commentary will attest.

In his session with me, Bradshaw invited a high school football coach who came to see him to stay and discuss strategy when Terry had concluded his session. Although they had never met, they spent 20 minutes conversing. When I asked the coach if he knew Terry before today he replied, "No. This is the first time I've ever seen him in person."

"I just love talkin' football," was Bradshaw's answer. In my opinion he could have left off the word football and he would have described himself perfectly. The man's got a motor for life.

Dan Marino

Hosting Marino in 1988 for one of his first card show appearances, I expected a huge turnout. I sold 350 autographs at the rate of $8 on any item, and actually sold more through the mail.

Dan is a "grin and bear it" signer with speed. In appearances he flies, limiting the conversation and keeping his pens moving.

He'll chat, but you'll get short answers. He'll personalize and allow photographs, but you can tell he's not overwhelmed by it. Instead, he realizes it's part of the process. Even though he's fast he'll maintain courtesy and politeness, often asking where signatures are wanted on items, checking for spelling, and responding to "Thank you's" with "You're welcome."

In public Dan is a willing signer, although it's usually one-per-person. He favors kids. He signs and moves on. The signature can sometimes be illegible, and at appearances it gets worse as the session progresses. He'll usually add a sloppy "13" under his name. He'll often refuse additional requests, saying he's already signed for the person earlier.

In my opinion, Dan's more business than pleasure, but he does take time for the fans.

Kareem Abdul-Jabbar

In a business that generally provides smaller turnouts for basketball appearances, Abdul-Jabbar was a great success. He signed over 1200 items. Kareem would only sign "Abdul-Jabbar" without his first name, saying this is his standard autograph practice. For a while in earlier appearances, he just signed "Kareem." He told me the only time he signs his full name is on his checks, although he has since done appearances where he would sign the entire name for an additional fee.

Kareem Abdul-Jabbar. The thinker, quiet type who is one tall dude. So tall he wants to sit when you do photos with him.—Photo by Joanne Thresher

Abdul-Jabbar has an intimidating physical presence. After all, he must bend to use doorways. He's doesn't like standing for photos, and instead prefers to take them while he sits and others in the photo stand. He's quiet, and appears often to be lost in his own world. He gathers his thoughts before speaking. You'll come away thinking he's really got a vanilla personality. He flatly refuses to sign his original name of Lew Alcindor, although many say they have obtained that signature. Even offering to pay extra got a refusal.

In appearances, Kareem keeps things moving, saying little and providing short answers. He won't personalize items, saying if he did it for one, he'd end up doing for all. Forget posed photographs, but he will look up after signing so a fan can get one in that manner.

In public, Kareem mostly refuses requests. If he does sign, it will be a one-per-person limit. It's hard for him to hide. To his credit, the signature maintains a consistency and neatness.

Two side items about Kareem. He grew up a Brooklyn Dodger fan and that can get him talking. Also, I believe he had a dislike for the late Wilt Chamberlain, as every time he had the opportunity to sign an item with both of their faces in the photo, he signed across Wilt's face, regardless of the amount of space available. It didn't seem to make sense.

Willie McCovey

A toughie in public, Willie will usually refuse or tell you he'll catch you later. In appearances, he'll do the minimum and just sign away. He'll do a personalization if pressed, but you can tell he dislikes them. For photos, forget posed shots, although he'll look up on occasion. His signature can be neat or sloppy, pending his mood at the moment.

Willie is quiet and provides short answers. You're not going to get long stories with him. He prefers to say little, although you won't hear any bad-mouthing or criticism. Needless to say, Willie won't win any personality contests. He complains of claustrophobia at appearances, so it's best to let him go at his own pace. Physically, McCovey is tall man with many ailments, including bad knees that slow his walk. He never appears to be in a hurry, mainly because of his aches and pains.

My guess is that Willie is also a silent jokester. When asked to sign a ball with ROY '58 (Rookie of Year 1958), it came out "ROY 1968." Assuming it was correct, we placed the ball back into its box, ready to mail. When the customer called a few days later telling of the error we were shocked. We issued a refund. Willie had put one over on us.

Nolan Ryan

I've never hosted Ryan in an appearance, but have crossed paths with the all-time strikeout king on many occasions. Ryan does about one appearance per year, usually for a promotional outfit in New York. His fee is high, discouraging others.

In the heyday of his career when he was approaching the all-time record, demand was incredible. But Ryan usually stopped and signed one for each person, limiting photos and personaliz-ations, but making sure all were satisfied. He would limit the con-versation, preferring instead to stick to the signing. He'll remind you that it's one-per-person when he's signing in crowds, and even when asked for a second one, he'll kindly tell you he's provided one, and that's the rule.

Ryan always takes his time, providing everyone with a clean, clear autograph. If he knows he is signing a more valuable piece, Ryan has the courtesy to check with the requestor for the place-ment of his signature. He has a politeness about him, saying "Thank you" and "You're welcome" often. If he sees a crowd, he'll stop and sign rather than avoid the situation. If the crowd is small, you may even get multiples, depending on his mood. Retirement has with-drawn Ryan pretty much from public view, and I think he prefers it that way.

Nolan remains the quiet country boy who made it big. He's never forgotten his roots, and realizes that it's part of the price of fame to sign and take time for the fans.

Tim Raines

He's a quiet sort who just goes about his business. He was much that same way on the field, and in fact, could end up in Cooperstown. Hosting him in 1995, it was easy to see that the old drug and party animal was gone and now replaced by the dedicated family man. He's a willing, cooperative signer in public and private. He'll personalize, allow photos, and converse, although his nature is to provide short answers. He's a fast signer, says little, and prefers to concentrate on the task.

Raines has a natural sloppy autograph, but it remains remarkably consistent no matter how many he signs. Multiples are possible in public. He realizes it is easier to sign than to avoid the confrontations. Kids are a priority in crowds. When Raines was with the Yankees, he was one of the better signers on a team of toughies.

Talking baseball with Raines will bring incredible recall of places, persons and dates. You won't hear much negativity or criticism: rather, you'll sense an attitude that he's had fun and is most appreciative for the opportunity.

Raines donated the proceeds from his signing to a charity in his home town of Sanford, Florida. That says volumes about Raines. He's remembered his roots.

Moose Skowron

Prior to the death of Mickey Mantle in 1995, Moose usually came as part of the package when you agreed to have Mantle as a guest. This was due to the fact that they were close friends and Mick was trying to help Moose out.

Moose looks old school, but actually sits in the middle. He doesn't criticize today's players, even if you bait him to do so. However, he will tell you that the star players of his era would be much the same today.

Skowron is friendly and cooperative. Posing and personalizations are no problem, public or private. If you get him talking he's tough to stop, and much of the conversation will be old baseball stories. He'll love every minute of it, as he fits in as one of the boys. He doesn't have to be the life of the party; just a part of it.

The quality of his signature never changes. It's always written as though he was in a hurry and nothing fancy—much like his playing career. Skowron is one who enjoys appearances and remembering the glory days of the past. He likes being remembered.

Dave Winfield

Winfield's career of 20 years also paralleled the autograph industry. In that time, he gained Hall of Fame statistics. By the time of his retirement, the hounds had gotten to him. He's had no trouble refusing in public, limiting numbers when he does sign and avoiding the crowds. If he does sign, expect just one quick signature.

In appearances, Dave will personalize and pose, but he seems to be doing it more because it's part of his job, not his character. He moves quickly and limits conversation, giving short answers when he does reply. The signatures start and stay sloppy, and are sometimes even impossible to read.

Although he doesn't say much, sometimes his facial expressions tell the story. When asked about George Steinbrenner, he just shook his head and with a sly grin said, "No comment. Next question." When you converse with him, you'll see a high confidence level—almost a conceit. What you'll see is a true "grin and bear it" type.

Ozzie Smith

One of the nicest players who just missed my Top Ten Good Guy list. In public Ozzie will stop and sign, even taking the time to personalize and pose. I've seen situations where three or four players walked by a crowd, but Ozzie would stop. At times you could tell it might not be where he wanted to be, but he realizes it is part of the game.

Smith is the same at appearances, although a high fee limits them. He will do what is necessary to satisfy the customer. The signatures are always neat, clean and consistent. He'll converse and even joke with the audience, but it's always positive. You just won't hear Smith bad-mouthing anyone or using rough language. He is a modest, humble, thankful man who realizes baseball has been very good to him. Maybe that is why he has trouble saying no. For the record, I have seen Smith turn down requests, but it's usually for a good reason—he's in a hurry or he has already signed for that individual. Ozzie seeks out the kids in a crowd and gives them priority treatment. He's polite and even when he tells you, "No seconds," he'll do it in a courteous manner, saying he wants to try to get one for everybody.

I once heard Smith say he estimates he's signed his name over 10 million times in his life. It wouldn't surprise me if it's true. He's a class act.

Tom Seaver

Seaver is another who is different in public and appearances, although the best word to describe him is "fast." He doesn't mind posing and personalizations at signings and will even converse, but expect short answers so he can keep things moving.

In public, "Tom Terrific" will often refuse. It's a 50-50 shot depending on a number of factors like crowd size, his attitude, and the location. Tom will keep moving, so when you approach him expect to get your autograph on the run. His signature always has the same sloppily slanted, up-and-down look, partly caused by his haste to accommodate as many requests as possible. He doesn't mind putting what he sees as repeat or unreasonable requestors in their place.

Tom had a high opinion of himself when he played, and he still does. Although he has studied the game and passes on much of his knowledge through the broadcasting booth, he can often come off as a know-it-all. Seaver will joke and laugh, but most of the time you'll see him as more business than pleasure . . . much the same as when he played.

Red Schoendienst

Hounds changed Red after his election into the Hall of Fame from a nice guy to a somewhat grumpy old man. Once upon a time Red signed all, but no longer. Today he will often decline, especially when he thinks he's previously signed for a requestor. In public functions he'll usually sign, but takes notes of who you are so he'll remember to refuse additional requests. If he has a chance to avoid the crowd, he'll do so.

Red's history is indicative of autograph collectors. Prior to his election to the Hall of Fame in 1989, Red was largely left alone. After that he was a marked target, and within two years had changed enough that he felt he could refuse to sign. He often refuses autographs on bats.

At appearances, Schoendienst will do what's asked and seems to have a genuine interest in making collectors happy—at least for the first 90 minutes or so. After that, he seems to want to finish the job and move on. He'll personalize, pose and converse, but will keep moving. His signature has worsened over the years and become much sloppier.

Red's face will tell you when he's not happy, but he'll usually bite his lip rather than cause a scene. Baseball has given him many great memories, but don't expect stories and comparisons; he's not a storyteller or old school advocate. He's not a braggart—in fact, he's quiet, so don't expect him to say much. The hounds changed him. That's what making the Hall of Fame can do . . . toughen the skin.

Robin Roberts

Roberts is an easygoing gentleman. Cooperative, courteous, and polite, he's much the same in public and at appearances. Photos, personalizations, and special requests are usually no bother. He treats each item with care, and his signature stays much the same.

Conversation is no problem with Roberts, and at times I've seen him get so deeply involved that I had to remind him he still had others in line. He won't get up and leave even if his time is up, and will tell you, "Just let me know when I'm finished." In public, he'll stay as long as required to meet all requests. I've never seen him refuse an autograph, although I have seen him deny giving more than one in crowded situations.

You won't hear bad-mouthing or foul language; that's not his style. He's not old school, and when you talk to him you'll realize he has incredible recall for people, places and dates. He'll admit he's a fan of today's players, but doesn't follow the game with steady interest. Instead, he's enjoying retirement.

Now residing in the Tampa area, Roberts has done many events for charity, where he's made many more fans with his friendly, casual attitude. Best of all, it's no put-on. It's the real thing.

Enos Slaughter

If you want someone to play the perfect country gentleman, Enos is your man. He's much the same as Roberts with his country attitude, but with perhaps a bit more modesty. In public and private he's cooperative, friendly, and willing to please. Personalizations, photos, and small talk are no problem, although he's probably not going to carry the conversation.

Although shaky because of his age, his signature stays consistent. He won't rush and appears to concentrate on each signature, making sure he gives it full attention. Like Y.A. Tittle, he'll often ask requestors the origin of older, unfamiliar items. Time isn't the factor; satisfaction is. In appearances, he'll always wear a sportcoat and be on his best behavior.

When you discuss his era, Slaughter speaks with a humility that seems to always credit others. He'll occasionally acknowledge his greatness, but most of the time his attitude is one of thankfulness for the opportunity. He's another who has come to enjoy the appearances as a chance to once again stand in the spotlight and thank the public at the same time. You won't hear a bad word about "Country."

Willie Stargell

Growing up 20 miles from Pittsburgh in the 1960s and 1970s, I'll always have a soft spot in my heart for Willie Stargell. He was and still is a Pittsburgh hero.

Willie is temperamental. He can even be testy at times, especially when he feels the crowd closing in on him. In public he'll usually sign, but don't be surprised if he says no. He's not crazy about photos, claiming they hurt his eyes. He'll allow photos, but won't look into the camera.

At appearances Stargell is more cooperative, although the photo policy stays the same. He'll converse, but expect short answers. He'll take his time and give each signature the same treatment. His autograph remains consistent and has a slanted appearance. He told me he dislikes the name "Pops" that was given to him by former teammate Dave Parker, but he's learned to live with it.

You also sense that Willie enjoys the payday with appearances, but would rather be elsewhere. In public, the Pirate great realizes it's part of the job, but clearly shows that he considers the hounds to be pests.

Deion Sanders

One of the funniest scenes I've witnessed in autograph hunting took place in 1996 in Plant City with Deion Sanders. After exiting the spring training game after the fifth inning, as the stars usually do, Sanders decided to run and loosen up along the right field stands. As he ran the kids kept pace with him along the fence, yelling and screaming for him to give them an autograph.

When Deion ran harder, the kids did, also. Finally, after about 10 minutes he stopped to sign. A madhouse ensued. People came out of the stands to get into the mob. Adults started throwing kids out of the way to get to the front. After about 15 minutes Deion ran toward the clubhouse, leaving many unsatisfied fans behind. As he ran, he threw one of his batting gloves into the stands. It looked like a fumble as people went diving after it. A teenager emerged triumphantly a few minutes later, holding his prize in the air.

In public Deion will tease his fans, signing a few mainly for kids. If the crowd is small, he will sign one for everyone. His penmanship is close to a scribble, and often the "S" in "Sanders" is done in the form of a dollar sign. He usually refuses personalizations, but allows photos. He'll converse, but it's usually a short, sweet, very hip answer.

Deion has done few paid appearances, and most were to promote his rap music. In such appearances he would only sign his CDs. A former Reds clubhouse attendant told me that Deion is almost two different people. One is the shy guy who says little and prefers quiet time like fishing and relaxing, almost a loner. The other Sanders is the one the public sees. When the camera's rolling, so does Deion. The art of self-promotion was never done better. His conversion to Christianity appears to be real, as his conversation frequently addresses his faith.

Early Wynn

Another member of the "Grumpy Old Man Club," Wynn came to despise autograph hounds. He did all he could to avoid signing, and had no trouble refusing. In paid appearances he was much better, agreeing to allow personalizations and limited conversation. Like Stargell, he claimed posed photographs hurt his eyes, and would even ask that they not be allowed.

It was clear that Wynn did appearances for the money. You could tell his attitude was to get this started and over with. He kept a speedy pace, but to his credit the signatures stayed consistent—a neat, legible autograph.

In public, he'd refuse requests for more than one autograph, and would look you over so he'd spot you the second time. I saw hounds bother him so much that he'd sign in exchange for the promise to leave him alone. He'd let you know where you stood, and his tone clearly delivered his message: "Leave me alone."

Wynn tried to organize the efforts of old-time ballplayers in the last 10 years of his life to aid those less fortunate, and to help the players of his day get more recognition and financial attention. He felt the today's players did little to pay tribute to those who came before them.

This was one tough cookie, on and off the field. Autograph seekers, like batters, weren't among his favorites. His growl often kept the hounds at bay.

Ted Williams

It might be best to describe Ted Williams in two stages: pre-stroke and post-stroke. The pre-stroke Ted was always a willing signer and a gem at appearances. Things changed after a stroke in 1993. His son, John Henry, had slowly taken over the management of Ted's autograph affairs, and had become overprotective with good reason. Ted was used to being active.

As John Henry assumed more control in the late 1980s, it seemed Ted's fee was always rising, making his autograph more costly. Williams, Mickey Mantle and DiMaggio seemed to have a contest going about who could have the highest fee. Thus, Ted was

Ted Williams with Sue and me (holding Andrew). This was the pre-stroke Ted. If you want to get him going, just talk fishing.—Photo by Joanne Thresher

always hounded for freebies. To his credit, he signed, although it was usually a one-per-person limit. He would personalize, converse, and pose. Occasionally, Ted would get frustrated with the constant badgering and simply refuse.

In pre-stroke appearances, Ted was a prince. He would personalize, pose, converse, and take his time, giving a neat, clean signature. I once saw him talk fishing for an hour with a requestor after his appearance was concluded. Ted might give you a wisecrack, but it was his way of joking with you. When he wasn't happy, he had no trouble voicing it. Whatever he felt, he said.

After his stroke, Ted's physical limitations made it difficult to walk, and to write for longer than an hour. John Henry began keeping him out of the show circuit and public eye. He made only occasional appearances, with the understanding that there would be no autographs.

All in all, Ted Williams kept his composure and class—even when crowds were large and demanding—until his stroke took him out of the limelight. He is a classy guy, although feisty at times. I once heard him say after autographing a ball for a teenager, "Now don't sell this. I'll come and get you." That is Ted.

Warren Spahn

Spahn is a funny, personable guy who seems to enjoy the autograph experience, appearances and just being in public. He's a willing signer, and gladly will do whatever is asked. He loves to tell tales and to be the life of the party.

At appearances he moves quickly, but never in a way that offends the public. Sometimes he gets wrapped up in his stories and you've got to remind him there's still work to do. In public he's as cordial as can be, but you can tell he doesn't like to be hounded for more autographs by the same clientele. I've seen him make deals by saying "I'll sign all of these if you promise to leave me alone." You won't hear him raise his voice if he's angry; instead, he'll simply say quietly, "That's it—I'm done."

Spahn's autograph is consistently sloppy. It's not only his speed, but his nature. This is an athlete who has kept his roots close to the ground despite his success. He likes to have fun, and has a good attitude. You'll come away with a smile after a few moments with Spahn.

Johnny Vander Meer

Vander Meer lived in Tampa since the 1960s and I got to know him quite well before he passed away. This was a guy who might have come off as another grumpy old man—but in all honesty, he felt the entire autograph industry was out of hand.

Autograph seekers didn't bother him; what irritated him was repeaters who seemed to always want more. Depending on his mood, he'd either decline and say he had already signed for the person, or just sign to avoid a scene.

Vander Meer was able to make a nice additional income for his retirement by signing and making appearances, and at times told me he was still amazed that people would pay for autographs. At appearances, his health and age slowed him down. He would take his time to give a clean neat, signature and even personalize and pose, although his preference was to avoid it. He had trouble hearing and would give short answers to questions, but generally, avoided long conversations. At times it seemed like his mind was elsewhere, but that was his way of keeping his mind on his work. Johnny wasn't old school, although you could tell he resented the big dollars paid to today's players. He wasn't a big fan of the game, and his family seemed to be the primary focus in later years. "Mr. Double No-Hit" was one who wasn't crazy about the limelight, but realized autographs were part of the notoriety. He learned to live with it.

Carl Yastrzemski

Yaz has a vanilla personality that gives the impression he's a boring person. At appearances he'll personalize and pose, but don't expect a great deal of talk. He's quiet and says little, concentrating instead on just keeping things moving. If you try to force the conversation, he'll just provide short answers. When I hosted him, Yaz stopped midway to catch a quick smoke and a drink.

In public Yaz will try to avoid the crowd, and will sign most of the time. However, expect a quick signature and not much else. His signature always seems sloppy, and at times is almost illegible because of the speed at which he signs. You can tell he feels out of place in public, and it's evident that he'd rather not be there. In most cases, Yaz will sign a few autographs, then leave. Forget multiples; you'll usually get your single signature on the run, anyway.

Hoyt Wilhelm

A classy guy at his best in public and at appearances, he signs willingly and does what's asked of him. He'll even sign multiples, unless the crowd is large. He has a naturally sloppy signature despite being a slow mover who doesn't worry about time. He even wears sporty clothes to his signings, and arrives early to make sure he represents himself well.

Hoyt fits in at any situation, and can spin baseball yarns with the best of 'em. The only problem is that he takes forever to get to the point. You won't hear him being critical of others. He seems to enjoy the opportunity to stand out in the crowd. In his case, it might be in appreciation for finally making the Hall of Fame. He's another who's had the chance to put a few dollars in the bank for his appearances, but in his case, he earns his keep by being such a good guy.

Earl Weaver

Despite his need to take a break for a smoke at appearances, Earl is another who has adapted well to the signing game. He'll say what's on his mind, even if it comes out as critical or sarcastic. The signature starts out in his usual poor penmanship and worsens as the signing progresses, although it remains legible.

As a show signer he does what's requested, but moves fast. Conversation brings quick, short answers. He pays attention to the time, even reminding the promoter when his time is almost up. Earl can joke and even avoid controversial subjects with an answer like, "I'm not gonna touch that one."

In public Earl will usually sign, but expect only one autograph. He can refuse if the mood strikes him, or if he feels the crowd closing in. Since his election, Earl has also capitalized on the collectibles craze by signing at three or four shows per year. He does what's asked and realizes it's part of the autograph game. He plays it well.

Tiger Woods

Tiger represents the new breed of famous athlete. He doesn't need to do shows and signings due to healthy endorsement contracts. He has bodyguards and is provided with security at events.

When Tiger does sign, it will be programs and hats—not photos, magazines, or items that would be defined as memorabilia and increase dramatically in value. He doesn't want to personalize and pose; the aim is to move fast and scribble out as many as possible. Conversation is kept to a minimum in an effort to satisfy demand. If asked, he will occasionally personalize those more valuable items rather than make a scene.

Because of security, autograph opportunities will be rare, though sometimes he'll sign for as long as 30 minutes on practice days. In actual tournament play, forget it—he's all business. He doesn't need to sign; his image is formed from the glowing media lovefest with this new kid on the block.

In all fairness, his drawing power can cause a mob scene. Most of the time, however, he's going to sign a minimal number and carefully watch what he does sign. The hounds know hunting Tiger can be a wasted day with no success. He's becoming a master of the word "no." The crowds make it tough.

Musician Joe Walsh

I include the *Eagles* guitarist because of his long affiliation with the MLBPAA annual Festival of Baseball celebration in St.

Petersburg, Florida. Joe came in with fellow *Eagles* guitarist Glenn Frey in 1993 to spend much of the weekend hanging out with about 40 ex-major leaguers. He liked it so much that he's returned about five times since then, and developed friendships with many of the players.

Joe has changed much since his radical party animal days of the 1970s. He still likes to party, but without the rowdiness. Instead, he just seems to enjoy the company. He's much quieter than you would imagine, especially when no alcohol is present.

Walsh is a willing signer, doing just about anything that's asked. Personalizations, photos, conversation, and multiples are no problem. He's always donated his signing fees to the alumni charities. His attitude in both public and appearances is much the same. His signature remains consistent and has a wild flair and backward slant to it. He handles items with care and seems glad to oblige.

At times he'll look at items with amazement, as though they represent a past life. Today, he looks more like an accountant than a rock star. As for the athletic skills he's displayed a few times in the Old-Timer games, it's easy to see why he chose the guitar. But he likes being one of the guys—and you can tell that the players enjoy his company, too.

Joe represents the fact that sometimes an icon's image differs —or quietly changes over time—from the real thing. Ask him for an autograph today and he's likely to reply, "Sure!" . . . not something rougher, like you'd have heard once upon a time.

Joe is one cool dude.

Now on to the guy who was the greatest hobby draw of all and the king of sports collectibles. Mickey Mantle was "THE MAN."

Chapter 7

Mickey Mantle

A few years back, at a sports collectible show, a number of dealers got into a discussion on creating a monetary currency for the sports industry. Names were tossed about concerning who would represent each dollar level. Names like Sy Berger, the Topps® Company official; Dr. James Beckett, who wrote the first card price guide; and Bob Lemke, who at that time was the publisher of *Sports Collectors Digest*, are considered front runners.

However, all agreed that one name stood out above all others —Mickey Mantle, who commanded a ten or twenty dollar denomination. Mantle cards, items, and autographs were always in demand. In the late 1980s, "the Mick" was the king.

Pressley told me when I first scheduled Mantle for an appearance, "You'll see how popular he is." Having hosted so many other famous athletes I laughed. He was right: no one has ever caused the interest and chaos that the Mick did in 1992.

On a ten-point scale of interest, I'd give Mantle a 20. Second would probably be Mays and Henderson, who would tie with a 10. For Mickey's appearance I sold all 1400 tickets (700 per day) for $30 or $35 each, and could have sold hundreds more. My phone rang non-stop with people wanting to send items or buy tickets.

After leaving my house one morning about 9 a.m., I returned at 3 p.m. to find 58 messages and an answering machine that had run out of tape. Calls came from 6 a.m. until midnight asking, "How can I get tickets?" and, "Can I mail you items?" It was non-stop.

In 1985, Greer Johnson began managing Mantle's appearances. She ran a tight ship—spelling out all the rules, a payment schedule that generally required full payment before Mantle got on the airplane, and the contractual amenity that she come along to

supervise the signings. Basically, Mantle would show and sign; she took care of the rest.

The first time I was exposed to Mickey's drawing power was in Charlotte, North Carolina, in 1985. Mantle sold out of 1000 autographs at $10 each. The line seemed to stretch for miles. Standing by the stage area, I watched Mickey plowing through the autographs, yet still taking his time to provide a clean, neat signature and some chit-chat. Like a skilled politician he shook hands, held babies and smiled. It was almost like Mantle couldn't believe the attention. There were no complaints from the long line of waiting people.

Many times over the years in various sports collectible publications, Mantle was named in polls as one of the top "nice guy signers." The hobby couldn't get enough of the Yankee great. He seemed to maintain that Oklahoma boyhood charm while being the big city hero.

As the hobby went into the 90s, Mantle remained a target. His autographs sold quickly, so the hounds always were chasing him. If the crowds were small Mickey would sign one for each, but he knew in larger crowds that if he started signing, he might never finish. He often carried pre-signed cards that he handed out in such situations.

Mantle's place in the hobby paralleled the growth of the business. In 1985 a signature cost $10 per item, but by 1992, it had risen to $35. As time went on, more restrictions were added. Items such as bats, gloves, authorized photos, jerseys, statues, and homemade artwork were eliminated from signings. Part of the contract required promoters to list forbidden items in their pre-event advertising.

In 1993, Mantle signed a reported $3 million per year exclusive contract with the Upper Deck® Co. The company raised his appearance fee to $50,000 for 800 autographs, which meant the promoter was into Mantle for $62 per autograph. A new level had been reached. The question was whether the public would now support Mantle and Upper Deck® at a fee that had instantly doubled.

One of the appearances Mantle did for Upper Deck® took place on March 27, 1993 in St. Petersburg, Florida on behalf of local bakery owner and boxing promoter Phil Alessi, Jr. Alessi had called me asking for assistance in coordinating a sports collectible show at St. Petersburg's Vinoy Park. He wanted to bring in a guest signer.

He asked me for my biggest draws ever and I told him Mickey was the king, but probably would not a wise decision to bring him back so close to his appearance the year before. But Alessi, well known in the Tampa Bay area, wanted to make a huge splash and refused to listen to reason. After Alessi signed a contract with Upper Deck® for Mantle to appear for that 1993 appearance, I had bad vibes for two reasons: first, the price for an autograph had more

than doubled, and second, there might be much less demand after signing 2800 (1400 in public, 1400 in private) items just a year earlier. Even with these reservations, I agreed to assist in promotion of the appearance and to run the autograph session.

Since we had pre-sold tickets, I knew demand wasn't going to reach 300; the question was what to do about the other 500 we might have left. I advised Phil to order 400 extra baseballs and extra photographs to fill out the signing. Unlike the year before, there seemed little interest, and an almost an indifference to Mantle's appearance.

Mantle arrived at the show, but this time without Greer Johnson. Instead, he was accompanied by a representative from Upper Deck® to count autographs and assist. After exchanging pleasantries, we began sharply at 1 p.m. As we started, we had sold just over 225 items to the public and another 75 to dealers in side deals. We were about 450 short of a profit, and the size of the crowd indicated there wouldn't be many more sold.

Since it was his first appearance with Upper Deck®, you could see he felt strange without Greer. He kept his usual pace, but limited his conversation. He seemed in a more serious mood than the year before. There was less joking and more business. The missing element was Greer, his security blanket.

Interestingly, *The Tampa Tribune* and *St. Petersburg Times*, two local newspapers with a total circulation of over 550,000 households, showed up for a story. Reporters interviewed people who had paid the fee, noting the doubling of Mantle's fee from the previous year.

The stories that came out the next day provided many observations, but noted the lack of signatures sold and apparent lack of public interest. The tone of the articles seemed to portray Mantle as greedy, and those who bought the signature as stupid for paying that much. The fact was, like it or not, that was the new standard for Mantle autographs and without paying it, you were unlikely to get one. As *The Tampa Tribune* article noted, "A hero is a hero, but business is business."

We struggled to sell 275 items to the public, another 100 to dealers and had Mantle autographed about 25 photographs and 400 baseballs to complete the signing. My intuition had been correct. My phone clearly indicated the lack of interest to this repeat appearance.

What a difference a year and another $40 had made. As Mickey left, I think even he sensed the lack of interest, saying in his country sort of way, "I wish a few more people had shown up." For a man used to sellout crowds, this had to come as a surprise.

Talking with a few hounds afterward I searched for answers. Some common quotes: "He was just here last year and signed a ton then—there just wasn't much demand left." The price increase seemed to anger others. The long time collectors, remembering the $10 Mantle signatures from just six years ago, felt betrayed.

One collector compared it to the king who doubles your taxes on short notice. "It looks greedy, regardless of the reason," he told me. "Collectors don't care about fees and rights; they just want a fair charge. This was too much."

In a hobby that had been in a slump because of overproduction, forgery, fee increases, and a number of other reasons, Mantle's second appearance seemed to fit right in with the downside.

Mantle remained with Upper Deck® until his death in 1995. He collected a reported annual fee of $2 million per year after the $3 million first year. The company marketed his autographs on many items, and "rented" him out to promoters two or three times per year in an attempt to regain their investment. Alessi did regain much of his investment, selling baseballs and photographs slowly to dealers and collectors in the next two years. When news broke of Mantle's hospitalization, Phil was deluged with offers to buy the rest. These sales took the appearance from a loss to a break-even proposition.

In public Mantle tried to avoid the crowds, telling me, "If I sign for one, I gotta sign for everyone—and that might take me all day." That's why he carried pre-signed or facsimile stamped items for distribution.

Mantle had a talent for telling collectors and dealers apart. I've heard him joke, "I know you're going to sell this, but I'll sign it if you just don't ask me again." That was easier in Mickey's eyes than being hounded. If you trapped him at a golf, charity, or other public event he would sign, but it was definitely one per customer. In such outings you always saw him with a drink in his hand and the life of the party. He liked to have fun. You always found a crowd around Mantle.

You rarely saw him without an alcoholic beverage, although his family and Johnson tried in the last few years to slow Mantle's drinking. The damage of long years of hard living and partying had taken their toll. At his second appearance he nursed bottled water during the signing. We discussed his health and he told me he was trying to drink less, eat better, walk and exercise more—although injured knees made it difficult. Mantle had always worried about dying young, since it ran in the family.

When Mantle received a liver transplant and bought a few more days of life in 1995, the demand for his autograph radically increased. Dealers, sensing the usual jump in value upon one's death, didn't mind paying the $75. In Mickey's final public appearance at the hospital he declared, "I'm no hero. Don't do what I did," referring to years of alcohol abuse.

One year after his death, an autographed Mantle baseball was selling for $175–$200. It was obvious the public still loved him—but then Mickey was easy to love. He always seemed to be looking for the next laugh. Many times he'd generate it with a practical joke or wisecrack. Around Greer he was more serious. He followed most sports—especially baseball—with more than casual interest, and conversation often went in that direction. He liked the old school but respected today's players though he would often joke about their salaries.

Mantle seemed to relish his privacy in later years, when golfing and fishing were his escapes. He appeared to avoid the limelight and autograph appearances were among the few times he was seen. He traveled between Atlanta (Greer's place) and his Dallas home. The knowledge of two women in Mantle's life (his wife and Greer) were unknown to most; his private life didn't seem to matter, the public still worshiped him.

On November 22, 1997, Leland's, a New York-based sports collectible dealer of higher quality memorabilia, auctioned off 200 Mantle items from Greer Johnson's private collection. A total of $541,880 was raised through the sale of 197 of the 200 items. Over 700 persons attended the live event at the New York City's Southgate Tower Hotel. Prior to the auction, Mantle's estate had filed suit to stop the event, declaring many of the items in the auction were too personal or actually belonged to the estate. A total of 33 items were withdrawn before the auction and returned to the estate.

There are numerous theories why Mantle had such popularity. The public admired his grin and country attitude. He played on numerous winning teams, both the nation's most-admired and hated. He was the first superstar of the television generation. Mickey always seemed to be having a good time. It didn't hurt that he could hit the ball a mile, too.

"He just came along at a time when television coverage took hold," said Schnorrbusch. "He just always seemed to be playing in a World Series. Most of all, he was a true Yankee. Fans just fell in love with him. The result was that when that generation grew up, they still had Mantle as one of their heroes."

Although Hank Aaron and Willie Mays were considered better all-around players, they seemed only a fraction as popular as Mantle. Many of the reasons are obvious: New York vs. San Francisco or Atlanta, World Series appearances, attitudes, personalities . . . even color. While Mays and Aaron were tough autographs who often scribbled their signatures, Mantle always did a slow, neat signature. Mantle seemed to wear his success well, although his popularity befuddled even him.

"Mays and Aaron were twice as good as I was," he once told me. "People seem to hold me in a higher regard now than when I played. I've never figured it out."

Mickey didn't hide, although he liked his privacy. While a public appearance might turn into a signing session, he would still do charity events, fantasy camps, golf outings, and banquets. He still accommodated requests, although he made it a point of one only. He realized it was part of the celebrity deal. Among the common people, Mickey could joke, laugh, converse or just listen. He was never rude, although a snappy quick-witted answer often came. When I introduced him to a blind collector, Mantle asked him if he drove to the show. Larry Powell of Winter Haven seemed taken back with Mick's comment, but answered the Yankee great with a serious, "No, I had a friend bring me." Mantle's next line was "Well you couldn't drive any worse than the people around here. There's a lot of them that must think they're on the NASCAR circuit."

Mantle graciously signed Powell's item, posed for a photo, shook his hand and thanked him for coming. His joking spirit gave you a smile. He handled each item with care, made sure it was signed neatly as requested, and gently handed it back. Often, a request would be for a number or statistic with the autograph. Greer discouraged the extras, but Mantle often did such requests rather than refuse.

He was held in such reverence that at signings people would go speechless, shake, cry, stare, and sometimes talk endlessly. He always seemed to marvel at such reactions, but came to accept it. He often engaged in light banter to put the person for which he was signing at ease.

Mickey's goal was the satisfaction of everyone who came for the signing sessions, often using the justification that "a person paying for it deserves my best." Many times over Greer's objections, he would pose, shake hands, or engage in conversations. Greer often reminded him there were more autographs to do.

Although Mantle's health had been declining and he had tried to drink less and do light exercise, his hospitalization caught the hobby off guard. With limited appearances because of the high Upper Deck® fee, dealers hadn't had the opportunity to stockpile Mantle inventory.

The price of an autographed photo rose to $125 (from $75), while a baseball jumped from $75 to $175 after his liver transplant. After his death a few months later they rose to $150 and $250. The price now stands between $250 and $300. Today authenticity is a concern, as quality forgeries can be sold quickly in the marketplace. His slow, steady, consistent signature is an invitation to forgery, though few have been documented.

Dealers, promoters, and collectors all acknowledge the impact Mantle had in both life and death on the sports collectibles industry. The sudden price increase after hospitalization and death turned off many, and spotlighted another reason to criticize the industry. The industry was given another convenient excuse or reason to accelerate its decline—the death of Mickey Mantle.

However, with Mantle admitting on his death bed, "Don't live like me. I'm no role model," the Mick seemed to shine again even in his darkest time. Willing to admit his failures placed Mantle in an even higher standing. In a country that often gives its heroes multiple chances, it was just a final opportunity for those who loved Mantle to say he came through again. There's no denying his collectibles, as evidenced by the earlier figures, will always be highly sought and destined to always increase in value.

Through Greer's savvy marketing, perfect timing, and his winning personality, Mantle was able to not only make large sums of money by simply signing his name; he was also to become the king of the collectible world. There will probably never be another to rival his popularity. Only Michael Jordan would compare, and he doesn't make public appearances.

In an era where athletic popularity comes and goes and media exposure is relentless, it would be hard to duplicate such an intense, long-lasting love affair with one athlete. Speaking from experience, there was no better draw for me than the Mantle of the $35 autograph. It was a pleasure to have hosted him and to have seen him in action at both public functions and signings. The man really had a way about him.

Simply put, nobody did it better. Maybe he should be on the collectibles' industry fifty-dollar bill.

Chapter 8

Close Encounters on The Autograph Circuit

Here are some of my best stories, anecdotes, and most offbeat tales from autograph situations.

Louis Lipps

If you want immediate attention in a crowded situation, be lucky enough to be holding the player's first sports card before he's seen it.

In 1985 at the Steelers training camp in Latrobe, Pennsylvania tons of fans were gathered around Lipps, trying to get autographs. Lipps was the 1984 AFC Offensive Rookie of the Year. Approaching the situation seeking an autograph on a football seemed hopeless until I played my trump card.

A few days earlier I had received a pack of 1985 Topps® football cards as a sample. Like any good collector, I opened the pack and one of the cards was of Lipps—his first. As Louie signed for the public I grabbed his attention by yelling, "Louie! have you seen your rookie card yet? I got one right here," I said, holding it in the air. "Come over and sign my ball and you can have it."

No sooner had I finished the statement than Lipps slowly began walking towards me, the crowd with him. I handed it to him, he gave it a 10 or 15 second inspection, then took my ball and signed it. "Hadn't you seen that card yet?" I asked.

"No."

"Looks great, doesn't it?" I asked.

"Sure does."

He then continued signing for others, but I could tell the card had made an impression on him. As for me, I was able to make him happy while getting my autograph in an impossible situation. Moral: never underestimate the value of an unseen sports card.

Walter Payton

Talk about timing? It couldn't have been any better.

It was to be Walter Payton's last game in Tampa, and on this Sunday in 1987, I figured it was my last chance to obtain the signature of "Sweetness." Leaving my house at 7 a.m., I picked up friend Terry Black and headed to the Bay Harbor Inn (the Bears' hotel). We entered the front entrance of the hotel. Standing in the walkway, we saw Payton approaching us, carrying a cup of coffee. He had finished his breakfast and was apparently headed back to his room.

Acting quickly, Terry and I asked for an autograph—even pushing our luck with two each. Walter said, "sure" to our requests, signed the items, walked to a nearby elevator and the doors closed.

Other hounds soon joined us and couldn't believe our good fortune. "He has a habit of sneaking out side doors, jumping in cabs, and just keeping himself out of sight," one told us.

Leaving at 10 a.m.—after most of the team had departed for the 1 p.m. game at the stadium, Payton would not be seen again by any of the hounds.

As Terry and I replayed our incredible timing, we marveled at the fact that if we'd arrived 30 seconds later, we'd have missed the chance to meet Payton.

Sometimes, the extra sleep can cost you.

Jim Abbott

I've always had great admiration for Abbott, who pitched in the majors despite being born with only one hand. So in 1989 while vacationing in Washington, D.C., I thought I'd try to get Abbott's autograph at the California Angels hotel in nearby Baltimore. Positioning myself near the hotel exit and team bus, I was sure I'd eventually see the former University of Michigan hurler. It wasn't 10 minutes before I was rewarded.

As Abbott neared the bus, I approached him. I asked for an autograph on two baseballs, and to please personalize them to my two sons. I must admit I was curious how he would manage to autograph the balls.

Jim took the ball and wedged it in between his ribcage and the stump of his right arm. Reaching across his body, he wrote neatly and slowly. As he signed, I told him of the respect I had for his ability to overcome his handicap, and that it was an inspiration to many. He thanked me for the kind comments. Other hounds will tell you that Abbott is usually the cooperative, cordial type.

Abbott finished the ball, removed it with his left hand and handed it back. As I thanked him, he went on to sign a few items for others and then board the bus. Jim went on to pitch about eight more years in the majors, compiling an average career with few distinguishing moments. He deserved more credit for refusing to be beaten.

Fernando Valenzuela

In 1987, I started out at 4:30 a.m one Sunday from Tampa with the intention of reaching Vero Beach and Dodgertown by 7 a.m. The goal was to get there early enough to meet Valenzuela and have him sign a baby replica jersey my son had worn.

Arriving just after 7:00 a.m., I positioned myself between the players parking lot and clubhouse. At about 7:30 a.m. Fernando pulled up, exited his vehicle, and began walking toward the clubhouse. I approached him, holding the jersey and my Sharpie®. As he walked, I asked him to sign the jersey. It was one on one. Not getting a reaction, I repeated my request. Again, I got no reaction.

After a 40 yard walk, he neared the clubhouse door. Deciding I had nothing to lose, I spoke up.

"Fernando, I just drove two hours in the dark to have you sign this jersey," I pleaded. "Can't you take a minute to do so? It's for my little kid. You can sign it to him."

Suddenly he stopped and said, "What do you want me to sign?"

"This jersey." I handed it to him. "Please sign it to Matt, that's my kid's name."

Valenzuela took the jersey, placed it on a wall near the clubhouse door, and proceed to sign it. I spelled out Matt's name to make sure that it was correct. After signing it, he handed it back and entered the locker room. I'd accomplished my mission —but to this day I

Matt's Baby Jerseys—I drove two and a half hours in the dark to get Valenzuela's autograph and he almost dusted me off 'till I put my foot down.—Photo by Tom Bunevich

have to wonder if Fernando was just playing games, or if he would have obliged if I hadn't spoken up.

Ironically, in the next two years the Dodgers would block access to that lot and the clubhouse entrance, even resorting to a security guard. It was impossible to approach the players after that.

Eric Davis

Davis won the contest for "Best Excuse for Not Signing" one day while he played with the Reds. Approached as he entered the team facility, he offered, "Not now, I just got up and I'm too tired."

Asked on the field during workouts, Eric would lament, "Not now. I've worked up a sweat and I'm tired." At the conclusion of his day while leaving the facility, Davis said, "I just got done working out and I'm too tired."

It was obvious Davis was one tired guy and had worked the excuse to perfection.

Stan Musial

In 1992, Musial was slated to be the headliner for the Major League Baseball Players Alumni Association's Card Fair in St. Petersburg. It was the second year I had been hired to promote and organize the event, and with Musial having not made a local appearance in some time, I felt he would be a big hit.

Unfortunately, he never showed. His signing time was to have been noon to 2 p.m. It seems that only a few days earlier, Musial's agent had told a few of the Alumni officials that Stan wasn't going to show because of an upcoming paid appearance in Miami. That promoter had requested Musial not do the *gratis* appearance because he felt it would cut into his sales. Those Alumni officials hoped he would reconsider and show because of the heavy advertising campaign that had been done. Unfortunately, they failed to tell me about the no-show possibility until after it had occurred.

I expected Musial to show, had pre-sold tickets and even began to line up ticket holders. Since this show has an average of 35 signers, it's wise to keep things moving. At noon, Stan hadn't showed. 12:15 p.m. came, and I cautioned those waiting to be patient. At 12:30 p.m., I began to think he might be a no-show. I pressed the Alumni officials, who finally told me this had been a possibility all along.

As the crowd started questioning me, I figured I'd announce that it was now apparent something had come up and Musial might not show—but in order to be sure, we'd give it until 12:45 p.m. At 12:45 it was obviously time to face the music.

I announced we would refund money, trade it for another player's autograph, or even exchange the ticket for merchandise for the other signings. Reaction was quite hostile. Over 400 tickets at $20 each had been sold. People complained, wanted me to give them more compensation for their wait, and generally acted like jerks. Trying to maintain my poise and patience was difficult. I had those holding tickets form one line, then handled each case one at a time. My friend Joanne Thresher and wife Sue handled the refunds while I tried to keep the show running forward.

After about a half hour, things seemed to settle down. It was my first no-show ever. I had no contract to fall back on. I eventually calmed down and eloquently expressed my opinion to the Alumni officials, informing them that facing such a crowd was no fun. I was assured it wouldn't happen again.

In 1993, Musial did come back and do the Alumni Card Fair. However, by that time he'd done an appearance for Gary Nagle in Orlando and the demand was much lower. I didn't get a chance to talk to him that year, but didn't hold it against him. It was great of him to come back, though—just to prove he really would appear.

Since those days, I have learned much more about Stan Musial. I've learned he's a really down-to-earth guy and a willing signer who usually appears when scheduled. But one day in March, 1992, his no-show caused me much aggravation. It's not one of my favorite memories.

Duke Snider

In a time before NFL Sunday ticket, the only way I could watch my beloved Pittsburgh Steelers was to go to a local bar with a giant satellite dish. Finally, after years of coaxing, I convinced Sue that we should get our own dish. We decided to buy it after our annual spring training show a few months later. Snider was to be the headliner.

We probably overpaid for Snider, agreeing to a $12,000 fee for three hours. Logic told us that he still should be a big draw, because he had never done a local appearance.

Duke bombed with less than 300 autographs at $20 each—a loss of almost $7,500 when you figured in his travel expenses. The show broke even thanks to a large volume of dealer tables, but it was a lot of work for nothing. On a personal level, I saw my new satellite dish disappear into space.

Snider needed a ride early the next morning for his flight back to California. I agreed to pick him up at the hotel and take him to the airport. I dropped him off, thanked him for coming, and tried to maintain a happy face.

As I drove out of the airport, I saw an airplane streaming down the runway. I thought I saw a satellite dish sticking out of the side of that airplane. I looked again, but naturally, there was no such object. As the plane went skyward I said to myself, "There goes my dish on its way to California."

To this day, I don't own a dish and still go to my local Steeler bar. I wonder if Duke has one? I'll bet he does. He should.

Ken Griffey, Sr.

I ran into Griffey as he sat in the lobby of the Hyatt near Disney in Kissimmee, Florida in March 1987. My real target was Dale

Murphy. Since the Braves were staying at the hotel for a series of games in the area and training in West Palm Beach, I figured this was the chance to get to the two-time MVP. Griffey just happened to be a member of the Braves and, like any good hound, I came prepared with items for other possible signers.

I approached Griffey holding a card and Sharpie®. Before I could ask, he said, "I don't sign no cards. I'm tired of you people making money off my name."

"Not even for a person who used to watch you play at Donora High School," I shot back. "I used to watch you and Bernie Galiffa (the team's quarterback who went on to West Virginia University) play football."

Seeing the look in his face of disbelief that someone a thousand miles and 20 years away would know these facts, I waited for a response.

"Ya, I remember Bernie," he said. "We had a good team."

I smiled. "I went to Chartiers-Houston High School. You beat us something like 26-7 and you ran all over us. You had a good team and we weren't that bad."

Griffey shook his head. "That's right. We kicked your butt."

"Now, are your going to sign my card?" I questioned, figuring he'd relent.

"I still don't sign cards," Griffey declined again. With that, I finally gave up and walked away. A few minutes later I ran into Murphy by the telephone, and he politely signed a few items for me.

In 1990, Pressley, Paul Kinzer, and I hosted a reunion of the Cincinnati Reds "Big Red Machine" team in Tampa during spring training. I offered the story up to Griffey, one of the show's guests. Although he didn't remember the particulars, he confirmed he had not signed cards for a long time and does so now only on occasion. (Since he was being paid for the appearance, signing cards wasn't an issue for this show.)

To this day, I still get a charge remembering the look on his face when I mentioned Donora. It was almost worth not getting the signature.

Ken Griffey, Jr.

It was mid-summer 1994 when I received a call from Felix Valdez, a Miami area show promoter. Valdez wanted my opinion about bringing Ken Griffey, Jr. to a show in Miami, mainly because Felix was concerned about paying $60,000 (plus expenses) to Junior, his younger brother Craig, and their father, Ken Griffey, Sr.

I told Felix I thought it was big gamble: one that could put him out of business. Although he'd be guaranteed 1,000 signatures of each, he'd have to sell almost 850 autographs at $75 each just to break even. At that time, the $75 Mantle charge and the public's resistance were still fresh in my mind. I knew it would be a tough sell.

My instinct told me 500 was a safe number. The high charge would scare off and limit the number by collectors and dealers. Even at 500, he would come up almost $30,000 short. "It's just too big a gamble," I remember telling Valdez. "If you decide to do it, send me some fliers. I'll distribute them and even try to drum up some business for you."

Wanting to see for myself, I decided to take orders and attend the signing on December 18, 1994. Leaving Tampa early that morning with friend Ron Ludovico, we arrived at Miami Lakes Health Club, the location of the show and signing, about two hours before the start of the session.

After arriving, we looked up Felix and purchased 24 autograph tickets and items for the signing. I could see he was worried. He had stacked bats, photos, and other items behind the signers in an effort to make up the difference between the actual sales and guaranteed 1,000. The last I checked, sales were around 600.

The line moved slowly as the Griffeys took their time, often engaging in conversation with the public. In the line were people with one or two items each, but they also had demands such as photos, personalizations, and posing with children. After about two hours, the line slowed to only a few stragglers. I then entered the line to have my items signed.

Hanging around for about a half hour after my items were finished, I watched as the line died. On occasion, a paying customer neared the signing table. The count was obviously short of the necessary 850. In the meantime, Felix had his extra items signed. What amazed me even further was that few wanted Craig's autograph (as he was then a highly touted minor leaguer), and only a few more wanted Griffey Senior. They were priced at $5 each.

Saying goodbye to Felix, Ron and I started our trip back to Tampa. As we discussed the events of the last few hours, it was apparent that Felix had fallen far short of the required number to break even. Our estimate was about 200 short, meaning an estimated $20,000 shortfall.

Perhaps some of the table revenue, admissions, and future sales to dealers on those extra items helped close the gap. What was lost was all the work, time, and energy invested into the event.

As one who has been in that position, I can tell you it's an empty feeling. Ironically, Felix Valdez never did another show. My intuition was correct.

Al Lopez

One of the most popular questions collectors asked me during my promotion days was "Why don't you get Al Lopez for a show?" I tried, but he just wouldn't do one. At the time of this writing, Lopez is the oldest living baseball Hall of Famer. He lives in Tampa, where he is regarded as a legend. Getting him to do an appearance is another matter.

Al hates the whole concept of autographs. He understands his role to sign when asked, but regards the entire scene as one he likes to avoid. For a number of years he did one annual appearance for a New York-based promoter, and word was that the money was placed into a trust fund for Lopez's grandchildren. Al did appear once for a charity in Tampa but left, disillusioned when two of his requests were ignored: he didn't want to sign mass numbers for dealers, and also wanted security for the walk to his car so he wouldn't be hounded for more signatures.

When the underpublicized show drew few requests for his autograph, dealers bought the tickets and loaded up, knowing the demand was much greater than the supply. According to Al, walking to his car turned into a nightmare when more requests came. The combination of these factors, along with the disdain he has for the industry, cooled Al to any future local appearances.

Despite this stance, the hounds would get him at his home on Beach Street in Tampa. They'd go to the door and Al would usually sign, except for signatures on bats. People from out of town that were here for other autograph guests often made the trip to Al's home. One Miami collector who frequently came to town for my shows always made a stop at Al's home to get two baseballs signed. They would fetch $75 each in Miami, helping pay for his trip here.

Compounding the problem was Al's mail policy. For a number of years he eventually returned mail requests, but for the past five years Al has been sporadic in his response. At charity events Lopez tried to avoid the crowd and make a quick exit. He was quite tired of the whole scene.

In talking with Lopez, what seemed to irk him was the fact that most of these requests seemed to always come from the same people, and that too much emphasis on money and not enough on keepsake value placed on the collectibles.

"I saw where a Willie Mays ball was selling for $50 and one of me for $75," he once told me. "That's ridiculous. Mays was 10 times the ball player I ever was." The trouble was, Al, Willie did more signing—and in the laws of supply and demand, those who don't sign enough command higher values and prices.

Bob Feller

I hosted Feller more than any other athlete, at least 10 times. Over the years Bob has become more grouchy, although he's always accommodating. In one of his early appearances with me, Feller was winding down the signing session while two young boys were nearby looking at cards to buy. They were almost oblivious to Feller's nearby presence.

When I suggested to the youngsters they might consider a free autograph from Feller as a lifetime keepsake one of them looked at me and said, "He's just some old man. We'd rather have cards."

Feller overheard the conversation, then piped in, "Boys, you ought to take advantage of this. Someday I'll be dead and this autograph may be worth something."

They weren't impressed. They bought a pack of cards instead.

Don Drysdale

As good as my timing was with Walter Payton, I had probably the worst of my collectible days with Don Drysdale.

136

The Dodger Hall of Famer appeared in Tampa on November 10, 1991, as part of a show to benefit the Boys and Girls Club. I had brought him in as a headliner to join a few other local celebrities.

After the show, I had an extra 24 autographed baseballs and 24 autographed photographs. In the next year I sold about 6 of each. In June, 1993, I sold the remainder to a local dealer for a bargain rate of $10 per ball and $8 per photo. The charge had been $8 per autograph at the show.

A month later, Drysdale died unexpectedly of a heart attack. Dealers and collectors flooded my phone with requests for those Drysdale items. Because of his sudden death and the limited supply, the price quickly rose to $50 per ball and $35 per photo. Unfortunately, I had none remaining.

That year I was asked at least a hundred times for Drysdale items. It may sound morbid to profit from death, but it's also a rule in the business. Then again, if we all knew what awaited us, we'd never make any mistakes.

Early Wynn

Wynn was a man I came across many times, and he always had the same disposition: growl like a tiger, never sign easily, and you'd better make sure you don't ask for a second autograph.

In a Washington, D.C. hotel lobby, the hounds were all over the many baseball stars in town for the 1986 Cracker Jack All-Star Game. As the old-timers passed through the lobby, most were willing signers. But Wynn had apparently laid down the law of "no autographs," as the hounds just let him pass by.

Young Terry Kors, Jr., who was with me, decided to approach Wynn while he was waiting for an elevator.

"No," was Wynn's reply before Terry could even ask, with Wynn giving him a short stare through his bifocals.

Wynn must have wanted to play games with the hounds, because he continuously seemed to be in the lobby. Terry approached him each time he saw him, and each time Wynn refused and gave him the stare.

After about five rejections, Terry walked toward Wynn, while Early again waited for an elevator. Finally Wynn relented, motioning Terry to come to him. As he started to sign the ball, the hounds descended on him in an instant. In the span of 10 seconds, thirty people now gathered around the former Indian hurler. Wynn signed a few more, then the elevator opened and he ended the signing with an "I gotta go." We saw him once more that day as he left for the ballpark, when he again refused all requests.

I commended Terry for either his persistence or stupidity, as he finally got his man. Sometimes that's what it takes, especially for a guy like Wynn who seemed to enjoy a good game of cat-and-mouse.

Archibald hounded Wynn a few years later at an Old-Timers Game in St. Petersburg. After about five refusals, Rodney got Wynn one-on-one in a walkway at the ballpark. "I'll sign it," agreed Wynn, "but if you ask me again, I'll kick you in the shins."

At a signing session with me a few years later, we asked Wynn about the shin incident. "I don't remember it, but it sounds like something I might say," he said. He would sign a personalized photo to Archibald that day reading, "To Rodney, the old shin kicker, Early Wynn."

Richard Petty

A friend called to say that Richard Petty was going to be on the noon show on WTVT-TV Channel 13 in Tampa. I had a 1:30 appointment in Lakeland, about a 40-minute drive from the station, so I figured I could stop by the station before the trip and pick up a few autographs for my kids' collections. Petty doesn't get to Tampa much.

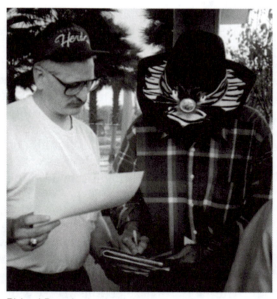

Richard Petty (under the hat) with Tom. Ten minutes later I crashed my van, $3,500 worth. —Photo by Bob Dell

When I arrived at the station around noon, there were a few local autograph collectors waiting outside the front entrance. Petty was there, and he told the crowd he'd sign everything on his way out. Figuring I had the time—and the fact I had invested in two photographs, I decided to stay.

At 1 p.m., the show ended. At 1:10 p.m., Petty exited the building and the crowd of 15 gathered around him. Taking his time and allowing photographs and personalizations, the King finally finished my two requests around 1:15. Knowing I had to be in Lakeland soon, I took off running for my van. As I reached the vehicle, a shower began. Rain poured for about five minutes, then suddenly quit.

On wet roads I flew, trying to make up for lost time. Soon, I was three blocks and one light from the Interstate. As I approached a red light and a huge 18-wheeler waiting for it to change, I hit the brakes. The brakes locked on the wet road and despite my efforts to pump them, they seemed to be ineffective. Going around the truck and through the intersection crossed my mind, but I didn't want to risk it. In a split second, it was apparent I was going to hit the truck.

Wham! I jumped out of the car to inspect the damage and make sure the truck driver was okay. He inspected his truck, which had sustained the blow with a steel bar, told me he was fine, got back in his cab and drove off. My front end had sustained heavy damage, but the car could still be driven. The repair job totaled $3,500.

This was the first accident I had since 1973, when I did $100 worth of damage to a vehicle. No more than five minutes after getting the autograph of the greatest race car driver ever, I had the worst accident I've ever had. Maybe his presence inspired me to attempt to drive faster. I ended up cancelling my appointment in Lakeland and taking the car directly to the insurance company and then to a repair shop.

Joking with A.J. Springer, my attorney friend, I asked if I could file a lawsuit against Mr. Petty for his inspiration. It seemed a natural. We never did, of course, feeling it would be a tough sell. Somehow, to this day, when I hear the name of Richard Petty I think of that slick roadway and crash. He sure made me the King of Speed.

Steve Spurrier

At a golf outing featuring Spurrier, the University of Florida football coach, and Bobby Bowden, the Florida State football coach, the hounds were having a field day. Bowden's a good ol' boy, generally signing all that's requested and allowing for personalizations and photographs. He plays the part well.

Spurrier has a sarcastic manner in autograph situations, usually inquiring what the item is worth or if it's going to be sold. He seems to revel in giving hounds a rough time.

"What are you going to sell this for?" Spurrier asked a collector. "Fifteen bucks," said the collector, "but we get $25 for Bobby."

Spurrier was speechless, and only could give that half-smile of his. If you know about the rivalry between the two schools and their coaches, that comment had to hurt.

Kevin Costner, Tom Selleck

Consider Sue's excitement when she learned earlier in the week that she would have the chance to meet and get her photograph taken with Tom Selleck and Kevin Costner. Both actors would be participating in the Major League Baseball Players Alumni Association Annual Old-Timers Baseball Game. Obtaining an on-the-field pass for the pre-game meant that Sue should be able to have her day in the sun.

Her job on the Friday of the game was to pick up son Andrew at his day care center about 3:00 p.m. and bring him to the show. I would watch Andrew while she and Joanne Thresher went to the field for pre-game about 6:00 p.m. Game time was 7:30 p.m. Bringing Andrew to the show, she told me that personnel at the day care center had told her Andrew had been complaining and crying about something in his eye.

Andrew was doing what any three-year-old would do. He rubbed his left eye and complained that it hurt. We saw it reddening, and Andrew's crying become more intense. At 3:30, Sue decided to take Andrew to nearby All Children's Hospital in St. Petersburg, thinking a quick stop at the emergency room would solve our problem. She could then bring him back to me, and go to the field about two blocks away.

Her call about 4:00 p.m. informed me she was still waiting at the hospital. Time passed and by 5:00 p.m. Sue still hadn't got to see the doctor, but it was apparent by Andrew's continued whining and crying that it was more serious than we thought and she would just have to wait.

As 6:00 p.m. approached, we faced the decision: Would she make it in time? We decided that 6:30 p.m. would be her last chance. Her call at 6:30 p.m. informed me she was finally seeing a doctor, but that the doctor had indicated it might take more than a half hour to solve the problem. So, giving the news to Joanne, I invited her to go to the field with son Matt. Matt was six at the time, and had no idea who Costner and Selleck were. The hope was that since Sue wouldn't get a chance to meet the two actors, at least someone should.

At about 7:25 p.m., Sue returned with Andrew. The youngster had a large patch over his left eye. The doctor said he had a scratch on his eye, applied some medication, and told Sue he would have to wear the patch for three days. The doctor said Andrew had apparently gotten some sand in his eye and by rubbing it had caused further damage, including the scratch. Light aggravates a scratched eye and thus the patch was necessary.

Trying to comfort Sue, I praised her for putting her son first. I surely would have gone, but was unable to leave because of the show and a number of signings. I tried to coax her into going after the game, but she didn't want to leave Andrew.

At 7:45 p.m., Matt and Joanne returned from the field. Joanne said the scene at the field was total chaos, with the two actors constantly being hounded for autographs and photographs. They were even having a tough time warming up because of the constant bombardment from people. Joanne said Costner even seemed to be getting annoyed with it.

Joanne soon showed us the fruits of her labor—autographed baseballs from the pair. She said she'd also gotten photographs of the pair with Matt, Joanne clearly felt she owed us something for the opportunity to get these two choice autographs. A few days later, the photographs arrived at our house. There was Matt, standing next to Selleck and Costner. Enclosed was a third photo of Andrew, crawling across a table with a huge patch on his left eye.

Andrew Bunevich with the eyepatch. That injured eye cost Sue a chance to meet Tom Selleck and Kevin Costner.—Photo by Joanne Thrasher

As Sue looked at those photos, I could see the disappointment in her eyes. Looking at the one with Andrew, I could see her sorrow for our young son. "I'm sorry," I told her. "That could have been you in those photos. But I'm married to a wonderful woman who put her son before a once-in-a-lifetime opportunity. I feel badly that it happened and I couldn't help."

Somehow, today those photos of Costner and Selleck with Matt have more meaning, but they will always represent what could have been . . . had it not have been for a simple grain of sand.

Cal Ripken

In the late 1980s before the Ripken mania days, the Orioles were staying in Tampa for a number of spring training games in the area. Waiting in the hotel lobby in the evening, I saw Ripken entering the front door with a number of others. Quickly, I ran to greet him. As I approached, I heard him tell his friends to wait in the lobby; he'd meet them there, and they could all leave together.

Luckily there were only a few autograph seekers, so Ripken stopped in the lobby to sign. Pushing my luck, I asked him to sign a ball and photo to my son Matt, which he did. Then I asked for an autograph on the extra photograph I had brought, handing it to him quickly. He signed it and handed it back.

With my mission accomplished, I left. Upon arriving at home, the ball and photo looked great, but the extra photo had an unusual signature. Pulling the photo out of its protective plastic sheet, I noticed the photograph didn't have an autograph on it; the sheet did. I had flunked hound basics: Take the photograph out of the sheet before asking for an autograph on it.

Al Hrabosky and Boog Powell

The MLPBAA Card Fair always represented persistence to get the mail order autographs done. In most cases it was easy: the players autographed the items during their signing sessions. For a few others who didn't make the signings, it might mean chasing the no-shows and trying to get the items signed before they left town.

Al Hrabosky always agreed to be a signer for the show, then canceled out at the last minute. Fortunately, since the St. Louis Cardinals trained in St. Petersburg and Al was one of their broadcasters, I always seemed to chase him down and get him to sign the items anyway. After two years of no-shows by Hrabosky, I decided not to take mail order for a third year. Yes, you guessed it: Hrabosky showed up.

Boog Powell was a show regular for the first few years, but you could tell by his attitude and behavior that he wasn't crazy about signing appearances. Then one year, Powell agreed to attend the reunion and play in the game, but not do the signing. However, we had taken mail order and wanted Powell to sign it rather than send it back and go through the time-consuming process of refunds.

Powell agreed to sign mail order after the game in the locker room. Amid all the chaos and other signatures needed at that time, we left a box of about 40 items near Powell's locker. Later we picked up the items and removed them along with all the other items we'd had signed while there, taking them back to the show headquarters.

Due to the large volume of mail order items—usually totaling over 1,000 items and $12,000 worth of requests—we kept all the items in a safe, out of the way place, so that only a few persons had access to them. It was Monday, two days after the show, when we discovered the surprise in Powell's box. He had signed the 25 photographs, but had not given them time to dry. Stacking them without the necessary drying time, the signatures had smeared and were ruined. We tossed the photos and later issued refunds for orders of Powell autographed photos.

Intentional, or not? We'll never know—but when it came to mail order for the alumni show, it was a tough enough job without the extra surprises. With as many as 35 guests and 1,000 items, it was enough of a task without the extra surprises.

Phil Rizzuto

He was scheduled to sign Friday of the show at 4:30 p.m. His plane was supposed to arrive at 3:30 p.m. and good buddy A.J. Springer was to pick him up and bring him to the show, about 30 minutes away.

As I looked out the large rear loading door of the Special Events Center of the Florida State Fairgrounds, I saw a cab pull up and Rizzuto exit the back door of the cab. Figuring I had better learn what had happened, I approached "The Scooter" and introduced myself.

Rizzuto said that his plane had arrived about 20 minutes early and not seeing anyone to greet him, he decided to catch a cab and come to the show. I invited him into the hospitality room, where I was soon to receive a call of panic from A.J.

"Tom, Rizzuto wasn't on that plane, and he isn't anywhere in this airport," he told me. "I think you better prepare to issue refunds."

"Just make sure you've looked everywhere—and if he's not there, we'll deal with it when he's supposed to sign," I told A.J. "I sure hope he shows up . . . I hate refunds."

"After you've checked it out, come on back and help me out. You know how much fun refunds are." I said, careful not to hint that our man was with me.

About 4:15 p.m., I met A.J. as he entered the building, pleading with him to produce Rizzuto. "I looked everywhere, even had him paged, and he wasn't at the airport," A.J. told me.

"Are you sure he's not there?" I asked. "Come on back to the hospitality room and let's make plans about how to handle this."

As we entered the small room, there was Rizzuto sitting in a chair off to the side, talking with others. He was oblivious to what was going on. Then A.J. spotted him.

"You think you're funny," he scolded me. "You knew all along, didn't you? I was really worried, and here you are playing games."

The session started on time, went well and Rizzuto was his usual accommodating and pleasant self.

A.J. picked up many of my guests throughout the years, and this was the only problem he ever had. I enjoyed the joke, cruel as it might have been.

Don Mattingly

One of the worst incidents I ever witnessed in an autograph situation involved Mattingly and the late-night hounds.

The Yankees, one of the teams with a large fan base everywhere, were staying at the Bay Harbor Inn in Tampa for a series of spring training games in the area. After a night game in Sarasota, many fans followed the team back to the hotel. With a large number of local hounds already awaiting their return, it was a madhouse at the hotel.

When the bus pulled up in front of the hotel just after 11 p.m., the crowd flocked towards the bus. The majority of the players saw what was coming and quickly got off the bus, dashing into the hotel and toward their rooms to escape the hounds.

One player who didn't move quickly enough was Don Mattingly, then a star first baseman for the team. As the crowd descended on Mattingly, he asked for some room. In a space of one minute, at least 100 people had gathered around him.

Don announced, "I'll sign one for everybody. Please don't ask me for any more." Seeing this, I backed off and figured I would wait. It was a sea of arms with countless hands stretching toward their objective. As people got their signatures, they retreated from the pack, shrinking its size.

A father and son team, apparently intent on getting more signatures, withdrew from the pack, circled it and re-entered at another location. Stretching their arms forward, they figured they could blend in.

Suddenly, I heard Mattingly ask, "Didn't I sign one for you?" There was no response. Don looked up and say directly to the son, "I signed one for you already."

"No you didn't," came a response. Then Mattingly asked again, "You're telling me I didn't sign for you already? I think I did. So here you go." He continued handing back the item.

The incident angered Mattingly and caused all conversation to cease immediately. From that point on, he said nothing—just grabbed items and quickly signed them. His usual quality signature now became "Don Mtty." He left in haste, obviously upset by the incident.

It's my belief that Mattingly, usually a cordial signer, had a right to be angry. Everyone gathered had seen the attempt at a second signature by the young man. After being kind enough to sign, unlike many of his teammates, Mattingly had been put in a tough spot.

It isn't always the athlete who's a jerk. Many times, the hounds are.

Ted Simmons

On the same trip that I sought out Dale Murphy and ran into Ken Griffey, Sr., I spotted Ted Simmons. Figuring he had an outside shot at the Hall of Fame, as he was still active at that time, I asked to sign a ball to Matt.

'To Matt, Best Wises, Ted Simmons," the ball says. I think he meant "Best Wishes," but no matter how many times you look, it still says "Wises." I hope this was a mistake; if not, someone needs to take Ted aside and give him a quick spelling lesson.

Fran Tarkenton

Before I begin the next two stories, I should tell you they involve hound Rodney Archibald. Rodney has been collecting autographs for over 15 years, often exhibiting a persistence that enables him to obtain the signatures of some of the real toughies. He has a "never say die" attitude that will make many celebrities sign just to eliminate his presence. I've seen him get very loud with celebrities, and even walking onto a runway to catch a celebrity on the way to his private jet.

One such occasion was when Viking Hall of Fame quarterback Fran Tarkenton was in town to promote his new book at a Tampa home show. Autograph hounds know how tough Fran's autograph is to get, let alone a fee of $40–$75 in appearances.

On the first day of the show, Fran Tarkenton was hit hard by the collectors and hounds. They had Tarkenton sign photographs, mini-helmets, and footballs. Few bought his book. On the second day, Rodney and friends arrived at the show early to get to Fran before word got out that he was signing all items. As Rodney approached Tarkenton, he saw Fran stacking his books on his autograph table.

Rodney politely asked Tarkenton to sign his items. Tarkenton replied that he was only signing his book and not permitted to sign any other items. Rodney pleaded that this wasn't the case yesterday; he had purchased his items just for this signing, and that nowhere in all the publicity did it say he'd only sign his book. After about 10 minutes of pleading Fran finally relented, telling Rodney he'd sign his items at the end of his appearance some four hours later.

In the next four hours, Fran told the countless hounds that showed up he'd only sign his book. All left without the signature, but Rodney wasn't about to leave without his autograph. As the four hours were about to end, Tarkenton got up from his table and went to a nearby security guard. His conversation involved pointing at Rodney and friends.

Fran then went back to his table, packaged up his books and began to head toward a side exit. Rodney and friends began to follow, until the same security guard stopped the hounds. When it appeared Tarkenton was out of sight, the guard told Rodney and friends they could go.

Rodney quickly took off in the direction of Tarkenton's disappearance and came upon him at one of the exhibitor's booths. Sensing Tarkenton was trying to give him the slip, Rodney quickly jumped in front of the Hall of Famer and asked, "Is it okay for you to sign now?" Fran said, "I'm sorry I can't sign."

Rodney shot back, "You told me you'd sign when your time was up. I've waited the whole time."

Tarkenton's response was to grab Rodney by the arm and repeat his story. Rodney only smirked and gave a disgusted look; his face seeming to say, "I'm not buying it."

Fran finally knew he was beaten and agreed to meet Rodney and friends by the rear exit in five minutes, even pointing to the door he would use. True to his word this time, Tarkenton stopped and signed after exiting the building. He limited the signing to two per person for the few that had made the wait.

Archibald's persistence had paid off, again.

Loretta Lynn (Not an athlete—just a good story)

Rodney has a guitar that he has Hall of Fame musicians sign. Loretta Lynn's appearance at the Florida State Fair on February 10, 2000 was a call to action.

Arriving at the fair shortly after Lynn had started her concert, Rodney figured his best chance for an autograph was to wait by her tour bus. A security guard told him it was behind the Entertainment Hall, the place of her concert. Going behind the hall, he discovered the bus was in a fenced-in area with no public access. It was time for Plan B.

Hanging around the rear doors of the hall, Archibald noticed an open door and decided he'd enter, stilling carrying the guitar in its case. As timing would have it, just as he entered, Lynn's musicians exited a nearby stage and walked directly in front of him.

Figuring this was his chance, he quickly got in line with the others. They walked about 15 yards around a corner and past a security guard into the backstage area. Feeling home free, he stopped and looked for Lynn. Another security guard approached him and said, "You guys put on a great concert."

Not wanting to make a scene, Rodney replied, "Thanks. It's been cold here, hasn't it?" The guard replied, "Yeah, it's been cold the last few nights." Rodney then thanked him and moved to another area, all the while searching for Lynn. He spotted her in a corner of the large room, posing for pictures and signing autographs. It was being organized by a long-haired man of about 40.

As he was patiently waiting his turn, Lynn walked away toward her bus. Trying to quickly follow her without making a scene, he was too late. Turning around, he saw the man who had been organizing the photographs and autographs.

"You think that Loretta could sign my guitar?" he asked the man. "Sure—but take it out of the case and I'll take it to her on the bus," was the man's reply. Rodney promptly took the guitar out of the case, handed it to the go-between, and moved near the door of the bus.

As he was waiting, another guard approached and asked to see his backstage credentials. "I don't have any." I'm just here to get an autograph," was Archibald's reply. "You'll have to leave," said the guard. "Let's go."

"Soon as I get my guitar back, I'll go," Rodney said. A few minutes later the man and guitar returned. After Rodney put the guitar back into its case, the guard escorted him out of the area.

Mission accomplished, but not without some luck. That guitar case might have bought enough time for the autograph.

Now it's on to some great tales from the hounds themselves.

Tom Bunevich

Chapter 9

The Hounds Have Tales

In this chapter, we'll take a look at a number of superstar athletes from the perspective of three long-time autograph hounds. They'll deliver their observations, experiences, and opinions of some big name athletes.

A.J. Springer, an attorney, will go first. A.J. is a collector and does not sell his items. He enjoys the hunt. He has been chasing autographs since 1984 and goes to hotels, airports, charitable functions, team practices, and just about anywhere an athlete with a desirable signature can be found. I've known A.J. to wait at hotels until 2 a.m., only to be refused.

Greg Kempton has been a hound since the late 1980s. Many of the items he gets signed go into his and his son's personal collections. He sells many more. He's willing to pay for extras on the spot and often inquires about them. Greg is an insurance agent and financial counselor.

Jan Moncol, also an attorney, is King Hound in the Tampa area. He collected autographs as a child in the 1970s, then rediscovered the hobby in the mid-80s. He sells the vast majority, but does keep a few for himself and his son. He is bolder and more aggressive than the others and seems to have connections that always let him know which athletes are in town and where. If Jan can't get an autograph, nobody in the area can.

• • •

Here's A.J.'s take on Wayne Gretzky, Michael Jordan, Mario Lemieux, Jerry Rice, and Tampa hero Warrick Dunn.

Wayne Gretzky

There is possibly no athlete that exemplifies how the growth of the autograph industry effects players signing habits than "The Great One." When Gretzky played for the Los Angeles Kings, it was rare that he would deny an autograph request. (He had not appeared in Tampa before then, since Tampa didn't have an NHL team until 1992.) He seemed to realize that as a superstar and the game's ambassador, signing autographs was part of the requirements.

As the crowds and demands grew, an in-person autograph became harder to get. Gretzky began the practice of moving straight to the bus with a casual wave. His trade to the Rangers toughened Gretzky even more, and in-person autographs were almost non-existent.

Wayne uses alternate hotel exits, and continues the practice of keeping on the move giving a casual wave, sometimes complaining about being asked so much for signatures, and refusing. On one trip to Tampa with Gretzky in town for three days, he constantly refused to sign. On the last day he greeted requests with, "Haven't I already signed for you?" Some of the hounds responded with, "When, Wayne? We've been here all three days!" They were still turned away.

It's common knowledge that a large number of autographs being sold as Wayne's signature are forgeries, so purchasing it is risky. In person, your chances are slim. If you want an autograph of the all-time leading scorer in hockey, the safest way is to order from Upper Deck® Authenticated, which has an exclusive agreement with him.

Michael Jordan

From the moment Jordan sunk the winning basket in the NCAA championship game, he has become probably the most recognizable athlete on earth. Six championships with the Chicago Bulls took it to an even higher level. This has made him the most sought-after autograph in the country—maybe the world. This means huge crowds whenever he goes.

Ironically, Jordan tries to sign when opportunity arises. You have to get him one-on-one. That's the tough part. Michael leaves through remote hotel exits and from the back of areas where he is appearing. Sadly, he must do this in order to avoid the huge crowds and potential mob scenes.

It was Jordan's first retirement from basketball that created opportunities to get his autograph at the baseball field. When playing in Sarasota with the White Sox for spring training, Jordan arrived early and sometimes stopped his car at the gate into the player's parking area to sign for those who were waiting. When another car came along, Jordan declared he was finished and moved on. When word got out that he would sometimes sign in this manner, the crowds even gathered the night before, staking out a spot to improve their chances.

Unfortunately Jordan didn't always stop, so a long, tired wait often resulted in no payday. Jordan often signed while on the field for warm-ups and practice, but the crowds were so large that only a chosen few would get an autograph.

Since leaving basketball, Michael has been a willing signer on the celebrity golf tournament circuit, but the large crowds and constant demand mean only a small percentage obtain a signature. If you can get him in a small crowd, he'll usually sign for all. "His Airness" will make an effort to sign autographs; it's simply a case of overwhelming demand. Jordan can size up the situation and if it looks like he can get things over quickly, he'll stop and sign. Otherwise, he'll look for a way around the crowd.

Like Gretzky, forgeries are a problem with Jordan items for sale. Michael does no shows, avoids the public as much as possible, and signs no mail. The best bet again is Upper Deck® Authenticated. It might cost a few more bucks, but you'll get the real thing without fighting a crowd.

Mario Lemieux

If you could use only one word to describe Mario Lemieux, it would be "class." Just like his on-the-ice presence, this same attitude also goes with the way he approaches signing autographs. I've often said that I have never felt better about being turned down for an autograph than by Lemieux. He doesn't make you feel inadequate or bad; he simply provides a soft, reasonable explanation as to why he can't do it at that time. The surrounding circumstances usually support his logic, such as a team meeting, or bus or airplane to catch.

However, it would be fair to say that the times you are turned down by Mario are far exceeded by the times he is a willing signer for autograph seekers. I've been fortunate to have had many opportunities to approach Mr. Lemieux for an autograph. One of the first times involved his team staying at a St. Petersburg hotel that did not allow autograph seekers in the lobby. After the team bus returned to the hotel and many players had left for the night life, Mario returned on another bus with a few of the team's trainers and coaches. Upon exiting the bus with many calling his name from the street about 20 yards away, Mario simply turned to the crowd, smiled, and waved.

A few moments later he exited the hotel and motioned everyone over to him to sign, right in front of the frustrated bellhops and security personnel. A lesser athlete could have used the hotel excuse or said that he didn't have time to sign for about 15 people. Of course, Mario has too much class for such a lame excuse.

When Lemieux was making his farewell tour through the NHL cities, he became an even more willing signer. When his team left the hotel for the last time, Mario went down the line and patiently signed an autograph for a waiting crowd of about 20. I happened to arrive after he had finished signing, and was inside a van waiting to leave. When I approached the van and explained my late arrival, he willingly took my photo and pen and signed it. That made me think even more highly of him, because he could have easily waved me away.

After the game, some of the hounds had learned that the Penguins were taking a commercial flight. As any hound can tell you, this means the players must walk through the terminal to board the plane. This provided one last opportunity to obtain Mario's autograph. When Mario arrived in the terminal, the hounds descended on him, but rather than refuse, he signed as he walked. I waited to the end and almost missed him as he started to board the plane, but he turned to me, signed a puck and smiled. I thought how honored I was to possibly be the last person in Tampa to get an autograph during Mario's playing career.

The positive impression my encounters with Mario Lemieux had upon me were quite significant. Having gotten autographs from countless numbers of athletes in the past 15 years, having a legend act in such a gentlemanly, unassuming manner was truly inspiring.

It has often made me remember an encounter I had with Jeff Query, then a member of the Green Bay Packers. Query would have a short and insignificant career as a wide receiver in the NFL. He was complaining about having to sign autographs for a small number of hounds in the hotel lobby when an assistant coach walked by and said, "Enjoy it now, Jeff, because one day you'll be begging to sign for them."

Perhaps Mr. Query would welcome those requests today.

Jerry Rice

With the San Francisco 49ers playing in the NFC western division, the opportunities to get Jerry Rice's autograph in the Tampa Bay area are few and far between. A number of years ago the 49ers played the Buccaneers, and a large number of hounds had staked out the hotel in hopes of getting Joe Montana's autograph. With every potential Montana sighting, there was movement from one end of the hotel to the other.

While many chased Montana, this allowed for a rare opportunity for a Jerry Rice autograph if Rice could be sighted before the mob had a chance to move. On this day there were a fortunate few who hung around after word leaked out that Montana had already exited a side entrance. They were rewarded when Rice came through the lobby. Rice's mood clearly suggested he was rather disinterested in the process and eager to get the job over with. Little was said—he signed quickly and moved on to the next person.

A few years and accolades later, Rice and his 49ers came to Tampa to play the Buccaneers. Montana was gone and replaced by Steve Young, who by now was the top target of the hounds. Rice was virtually impossible to get an autograph from as he ran from the crowds and appeared not to hear them yelling his name and asking for a signature. This even stretched to a walk-through practice which the 49ers held at the old Tampa Stadium.

Rice ran on and off the field, ignoring the cries of the small number of hounds. At the conclusion of practice, a usual signing time for most athletes, Rice quickly ran onto the bus while many of his teammates milled around, drinking fluids, and cooling off. Despite the pleas from the hounds to come off of the bus and sign, Rice didn't budge.

Rice's attitude reached an absurd level on game day. With the hounds arriving early in the morning and hoping for a Rice autograph, the wide receiver was nowhere to be found. Even as the rest of the team boarded the buses for the stadium, he remained unseen. Just after the buses left, Rice appeared and quickly got into a luxury car that streaked by the pleading hounds.

Hustling from the hotel to the stadium's player's entrance in one last attempt to get Rice's autograph, I barely beat his car. Moving near the vehicle as it stopped, I pulled out my mini-helmet in an attempt to send Rice a message. He sat in the vehicle for a few minutes (hoping I would disappear?). Finally, I positioned myself next to the vehicle.

As he exited the car, I politely requested an autograph, and he walked right by without even acknowledging my presence. Since there was another 70 to 80 feet before he would go through the entrance gate, I caught up to him and again asked for a signature. Again, no answer. To this day, I've kept that mini-helmet unsigned as a memory of the grand occasion.

It should be noted that Rice has become a frequent signer at card shows and private signings. The opportunity to get an autograph has become rather easy, if you don't mind plunking down the money. Autograph seekers should keep him in his handsome salary; Rice has parlayed quite an income hawking his signature, which goes in the $75–$100 range. It's evident he doesn't like giving freebies.

A final note on my encounter with Rice: Later in the afternoon of my constant rejection, he suffered a season-ending knee injury after a tackle by Warren Sapp. I'm not sure if there's any connection between him dissing me and his injury, but you know what they say about karma.

Warrick Dunn

No individual athlete better exemplifies the modern day athlete's attitude toward autograph signing than Warrick Dunn, running back for the Tampa Bay Buccaneers. While recognized as a player who would freely sign autographs while in college at Florida State University, his signature left much to be desired, as it resembled a scribbled "W" and "D" with a barely legible number included. It was also late in his college days that Dunn's disdain for autograph seekers became evident.

He would routinely sprint past autograph hounds at practices by appearing to have something more important to tend to. It's interesting that this practice has continued until this day, with the average autograph seeker frustrated at any attempt to get Dunn to provide an autograph or even slow down. It is interesting to note that Dunn did provide his signature for numerous trading card companies to use as inserts in their packs, for which no doubt he was compensated.

With the added publicity of being a star at FSU, Dunn's entry into the Tampa Bay area was greeted with excitement, and he was the immediate target of autograph seekers. His first contact with this crowd was at the Buccaneers' first mini-camp, shortly after the NFL draft. It was obvious he didn't relish the attention of being the number one target of the crowd. To his credit, he did sign autographs for many of the people in attendance on the first few days. However, it didn't take long for Dunn to begin blowing off autograph seekers, and generally avoiding the crowds which had gathered for the workouts. When approached for an autograph Dunn would say, "Didn't I get you already?" or just continue moving while occasionally grabbing an item to sign. The majority of requests went unsigned and in many cases, ignored.

Since that original mini-camp, Dunn's in-person autographs have been few and far between. When getting autographs used to be possible at the Buccaneers' training facility (the players had to walk by the hounds from the parking lot to the facility door), Dunn would usually walk by without signing, saying nothing.

Also interesting is that Dunn has not done any show appearances, although he did one private signing in a special corporate promotion. It would be easy to say that Dunn was in it for the money, trying to make his autograph difficult to get and therefore more valuable. However, he has done nothing to cash in on these circumstances. It's almost as though he doesn't want to sign for free *or* for pay.

In the private signing for the Checkers Restaurant chain, one of the Buccaneers major corporate sponsors, the strong promotion did its job. It brought a massive line to the Clearwater restaurant where Dunn did the appearance. Although the line was eventually stopped shortly after the appearance started, everyone who was in line got an autograph. He stayed longer than the scheduled time to finish.

A humorous side of the appearance was that many of the local hounds, knowing the difficulty in obtaining Dunn signatures, brought long-lost family members and friends along to load up on autographs.

There has been no explanation from Dunn or the local media on his constant refusal to sign autographs. It might be he doesn't want people cashing in on his name, is bored with the process, sees too many of the same people, or just doesn't feel like signing. Since it is likely he will someday do a paid appearance, this hound advises you to wait patiently for that day, then get your Dunn items signed. You'll pay for it since there's not much hope otherwise. Don't try the mail either, as it won't come back.

Another humorous side note is that when Leigh Steinberg, Dunn's agent, was doing a book signing, he would ask a few of his clients to appear with him at autograph signings. When Steinberg made a Tampa book tour appearance, Dunn and fellow Buccaneer John Lynch appeared with him. It was ironic that Dunn sat next to Steinberg—who may have advised him about autograph attitudes and appearances. When it came time for Leigh to add his signature as a selling device for his book, the act of putting pen to paper appeared easy and natural.

When Dunn was announced as the week's guest for a local radio program being aired at a local restaurant, the station went to unusual measures to announce that Dunn would not be signing autographs of any kind while there. While this was certainly a smart move by the restaurant and the station to avoid a large, demanding, and eventually disappointed crowd, it was a further irony that this occurred with the one Buccaneer who generally refuses to sign any autographs. Maybe someday he'll explain his side. Until then, the hounds will just accept it as a fact of life.

• • •

Kempton is next, and will feature Joe Montana, Brett Farve, Eric Lindros, Patrick Roy, Sonny Jurgensen, and Phil Esposito.

Joe Montana

I think Joe Montana was one of the classiest guys in sports during his prime. He was always serious when signing for the fans, rarely looking up and conversing. He would usually stop if the crowd was small. Very adamant about signing just one item for each person, he would bark and sometimes even politely refuse if you approached him with additional items.

In 1995, after Joe had left the 49ers to play in Kansas City, the Chiefs visited Tampa for a game with the Buccaneers. The hounds had a tough day. Very few people saw him once the team arrived at the hotel. This seemed to validate the new Montana attitude of "if you don't see them, you don't have to sign them." Nowadays, getting a chance to catch Joe one-on-one seems to be the problem.

Most recently, I met him at a celebrity golf tournament in North Carolina. As usual, once he was seen, he accommodated the hounds. He tried even then to remind people of his one-item-per-person limit, but the hounds simply approached him at another time or circled around the crowd. Not one to make a scene, Joe would grin and bear it.

Joe now does about two or three shows per year, with a usual fee of $100–$125 per item. You can play it safe and go this route, or go where he may be, but again you must hope you'll see him. He seems to have developed a skill for avoiding the hounds.

In 1992, I got two cards signed through the mail, but they were auto-penned, not hand-signed. I wouldn't try this route today.

Brett Farve

Much like his feisty personality, so goes the autograph world with Farve. He is one of the funniest players in sports today, and loves to barb with the hounds, giving excuses why he can't sign right now. They range from a simple "Got to go" to the truly imaginative. When he was in town with the Packers a few years back, he returned to the hotel from what was evidently a rather large meal, telling the hounds, "Sorry guys, I am *too* full to sign . . . I'll get you later." Even the hounds laughed at that one.

Although he's going to avoid the crowds, Farve will occasionally sign when cornered by a collector. I would, however, classify that as a rare and uncommon event.

Farve does one or two shows per year for fees in the $75–$100 range. He also has a private company in the Milwaukee area he does many private signings for which keeps the supply up, especially if you're willing to pay the price.

Finally, forget the mail route, as you'll get a rubber stamp for one item and the others returned unsigned, if at all.

Eric Lindros

Over the years, hockey players have become more popular with the hounds. The sport of hockey does not have the following of other major sports, and demand and crowds are less. In the south, hockey is less than a decade old. Therefore, there is less demand, so players of the puck sport are generally good signers.

Lindros is one of the best signers in the sport. Despite his superstar status, he comes across as a serious, polite, and accommodating person. A tough guy on the ice, he's a gentle giant off it, as you will rarely hear him lose his cool.

On almost every occasion at the team hotel he has signed for everyone, including multiples. He once spent a few minutes in idle chit-chat with my wife after signing a photo for her. She, like many of the other hounds, was impressed with his friendliness and calm demeanor. When the crowds are larger, he'll ask for a one-each limit.

The mail route is tough. You may get it back, but expect a long wait. Lindros has done a few shows with fees in the $25–$40 range. Overall, this is one superstar who has managed to keep his head straight and his feet on the ground. He realizes the autograph game is part of the deal, and seems to have it under control.

Patrick Roy

Roy has an attitude that falls between Farve and Lindros, but mostly I would call him a good signer. Mainly, he takes a businesslike approach to the autograph game, but sometimes he'll joke or converse with the hounds. He often gives the impression he doesn't enjoy signing, but is doing it because he feels an obligation to the fans.

I recall an incident in 1993 that might tell the story of Patrick. At that time, he was with the Montreal Canadians who were in town to play the Lightning. The team arrived three days early and players spent much time golfing, fishing, partying, and enjoying the Florida sunshine. On one of the days, the hounds patiently waited in the hotel as players returned from the day's activities.

As Roy arrived from golfing, he was sunburned and slightly tipsy from a few rounds at the 19th hole. With the hounds descending on him, Roy offered, "I'll get you after I come back down from a shower." This usually is the brush-off, so many hounds left. Those who stayed were rewarded about 45 minutes later when Roy came down to the lobby.

He walked right up to my table and sat down, promptly signed all items for everyone, including six for me. As we were all amazed that he lived up to his word by returning, little conversation was exchanged. However, as he started to walk away I noticed he had smudged the signature on one of the pucks. "Hey Patrick, this one got smudged—could you please sign another?"

He walked back to my table, looked at it and asked, "Why—are you going to sell it?" I told him I wasn't and he signed another, again reminding me about not selling it. Since then I have seen him many times and he has remained a good signer, although he's likely to limit the numbers nowadays.

Patrick is a surefire Hall of Famer on the ice and in many dealings with him, I've come to regard him as one off the ice as well.

Sonny Jurgensen

Not a big name to today's fans, but Sonny Jurgensen is one of my personal favorites. Jurgensen always makes the fans—and especially the hounds—targets of his affection and sarcasm. He does it in a spirit of fun. He typifies the adage that "his bark is worse than his bite."

Once upon a time, he just signed your items and offered casual light banter. Now he is the first to announce at a golf tournament that "Dealers are here. I need to sign for them." He seems to feel that everyone asking for autographs is selling them and getting rich from them. Today he'll sign, but not until after a short lecture about selling autographs and making money off them. I once heard him ask a 10-year-old boy, "You're selling these autographs, aren't you?" Meanwhile, he just kept signing multiple items for the youngster.

If you're not scared away by his outbursts, he'll usually sign all you want while puffing away on his cigar. He's a true peach, once you realize it's just part of the act.

Phil Esposito

Esposito has spent much of the last 10 years in the Tampa area in a leadership capacity with the Tampa Bay Lightning. I would regard him as a willing signer, and one who realizes it's part of the territory.

When the team was first founded, Esposito, as team president, was everywhere—and the hounds constantly took advantage of the free appearances. The first few times Esposito signed multiples, but later established a limit of one-per-person. You can tell he doesn't particularly care for the hounds.

Over the last years of his involvement with the team (1996–98), his appearances became less and less frequent. If you could track him down he'd sign, but he largely avoided the limelight. He did make a few paid appearances out of the state in the past few years with fees ranging from $20–$30, but there was never a charge in the Tampa area.

Phil will say what's on his mind, telling hounds in rough language that he's already signed for them. He's even walked out of a few appearances near the end when he thought the hounds were ganging up on him.

The one consistency is the quality of his signature. It looks nearly the same if it's the first or 500th at an appearance. His attitude might change, but not his penmanship.

• • •

Moncol is the final hound and will discuss Al Davis, Mike Alstott, Frank Thomas, Ricky Williams, Mark McGwire, and Troy Aikman.

Al Davis

Davis is one of my favorites, and a true classic. Currently, Al rarely signs autographs. My last experience with him was in 1997, when the Raiders played the Falcons in Atlanta. I traveled to Atlanta to get the Raiders, Davis included.

When the Raiders play in the East, they arrive Friday night for Sunday's game. My 10-year-old son Kirk and I arrived early Saturday morning. We saw Al several times during the day in the lobby visiting with ex-Raiders and friends. Other than an occasional member of the Raider fan club, when they weren't in the hotel bar, there were few autograph seekers around. I asked Al several times for an autograph that day and his responses ranged from, "I'm not doing anything right now," to "Later." I felt like telling Al "I know you're not doing anything right now, so why not go ahead and sign?" but I didn't, figuring it would blow any chance I had.

Al had a white stretch limo parked outside the hotel. Jim Otto, former Raider center and Pro Football Hall of Famer now serves as Al's personal bodyguard. Al was dressed in his customary white Raiders warm-up suit. I told my son to watch the exit and when Al left, to follow him and keep asking. When Otto and Davis headed out the door, Kirk quickly followed. My eyes tracked them to the limo, where Al stopped and signed a mini-helmet for Kirk. It would be the only autograph I saw him sign the entire time at the hotel.

Later, I asked Kirk what he said to convince Al to sign. He told me he'd promised Al that if he signed the helmet he wouldn't ask him again.

My favorite Al Davis story happened in the early 1990s at the Marriott on 17th Street in Ft. Lauderdale, when the Raiders were in town to play the Miami Dolphins. Al had signed for me early on Sunday, the day before the Monday night game. Unfortunately, Al had insisted on using his archaic Flair® felt-tip pen instead of my Sharpie®. When you use a Flair® pen on a card, the ink evaporates into the card, leaving only a faint signature.

I looked forward to Monday, when I hoped to get Al to use a Sharpie®. After the team buses had left for the stadium Al appeared in the lobby, kibitzing with some older ladies. Figuring the time was right, I approached him. He told me, "In a minute."

After about ten minutes, Al turned toward me and nodded. I approached him with my card and Sharpie.® Davis took my card, reached into his pocket, and pulled out his trusty Flair pen.® I vehemently objected and said, "Al, please use my pen." He ignored me and signed the card with the Flair® pen. As he was signing it, I blurted out, "Look Al, the autograph is evaporating!" Davis coolly responded, "Oh, f_ _ _." He handed the card back anyway. He's a classic.

A friend of mine ran into Al at the owner's meeting in Miami in 1999. He approached Davis and told him he was good friends with Sid Luckman, who is now deceased. Al responded, "How is Sid?" My friend said Luckman was fine, then asked Davis for an autograph.

"Have Sid write me a note and I'll sign whatever you have," said the Hall of Famer. It was more classic Al, one tough autograph.

Mike Alstott

Mike Alstott is generally a nice guy, and signs under most circumstances. As an NFL rookie, he signed everything with beautiful penmanship. After a few years in the league, he's toughened up. He still signs, but it's usually sloppy.

The recent success of the Buccaneers has made Alstott more of a Tampa hero and swelled demand considerably. Through the years, Mike has done a number of local appearances. For the past three years, he has hosted a weekly radio show during the football season at various Tampa restaurants. At first, the hounds bombarded him, but through the years there has been a "one-per-person if time permits" stance. Mike has come to believe that certain individuals have loaded up on him and made huge profits off his name. He seems to be everywhere, with many charitable causes and appearances. There's little question that his replica jersey is the number one selling sports item in the Tampa area.

The rumor is that Brent Tessler, his Ft. Lauderdale appearance agent and good college friend, has advised him to sign sloppily for free so that the quality autograph he provides at paid appearances will be worth more. However, Mike still takes the time to sign after games or practices, albeit a more hurried signature than a few years back.

One of the targets for Alstott's displeasure with the hounds is Kirk, whom Alstott has accused of being a dealer and selling signatures. Further evidence of his dislike of hounds is an incident at a charity golf outing last year when Alstott accused a friend of mine of "ripping him off by selling the autograph." He further asked the hound if he wanted an autograph, "he could read or an illegible one?" My advice to Mike is, "Don't sweat the small stuff." The few bucks being made off your signature is peanuts compared to our time invested and your income. Just go with the flow.

Frank Thomas

Frank Thomas, despite his superstar status, huge imposing size, and constant large demand, is one of the best signers in baseball. It's obvious that he believes it is his duty to the fans. I've seen him sign for great lengths of time before, during, and after spring training games. Even when he is a visitor, such as when the White Sox play in St. Petersburg, Florida at the Tropicana Dome, he signs for many people. Frank won't say much; he just keeps signing away.

The only problem I have with Thomas is he usually won't change pens. For instance, if he starts with a black Sharpie®, everything he signs during that period will be done with that pen, including balls, cards, programs, and photographs. He won't change, and instead just keeps signing away. With the large demanding crowds he usually has around him, asking him to change might jeopardize your chance—so take it or leave it.

Too bad that all superstars don't take a lesson from "The Big Hurt." Overall, he would be in my Top Ten Good Guy Signers in Baseball.

Ricky Williams

As a junior at the University of Texas, Ricky Williams was genuinely a prince. The first time I encountered Ricky was the at Orlando International Airport in 1997, when he arrived for ESPN's College Football Awards show. Back then he was still sporting his dreadlocks, but signed everything the hounds had in a friendly, polite manner.

However, things changed drastically during his senior year and his Heisman Trophy-winning season. Arriving for the 1998 awards show with his soon-to-be-agent, Percy Miller from No Limit Sports, he refused all requests. Later that night outside the ESPN Club at Disney World, he signed a few autographs, but his agent interceded often and stated, "He's not signing," as Ricky and his assistant walked around the area checking things out. In the past few years Ricky has done some private signings, and maybe the chance to cash in has interfered with his signing habits.

I think Williams can be a nice guy when he wants to, but the presence of his agent turned him into a non-signing machine. Perhaps, if all his "blockers" were this good, he would gain 2,000 yards in a season.

Mark McGwire

The first time I saw McGwire was during his rookie year at Memorial Stadium in Baltimore, when he was in town with the Oakland Athletics. He was a gracious signer and signed multiples before the game by the dugout.

One year later at Cincinnati International Airport, upon arriving for the all-star game, he refused to sign, stating, "I don't sign at airports." Exiting the same plane with him was Jose Canseco, Dennis Eckersley, and Harold Reynolds, all of whom graciously signed for the hounds.

As Reynolds signed for me, he turned to McGwire who was standing next to him at the baggage claim, and said, "I guess we'll be doing a lot of this for the next few days." McGwire shot back, "Not me."

McGwire has appeared to lighten up some in the past few years, although the barrage from the home run derby assault has created incredible demand. McGwire did appearances earlier in his career, but has probably done only one private signing in the last five years. He's also been critical of the autograph industry as a whole, calling most of the autographs being sold forgeries.

Kirk got him in spring training of 1998 when he returned to the hotel after a game with the Devil Rays in St. Petersburg. The next morning, though, he refused to sign at the hotel, saying, "It's too early." Sometimes when he signs in public, he'll insist on personalizing.

"Big Tweet" has gotten into the habit of signing a few autographs before games, although demand is overwhelming. He goes to the Frank Thomas one pen school, however, and signs everything with it, rapidly moving from one item to another with little break or chatter in between. My guess is that he's not crazy about the autograph game, but views it as one of those necessary evils of life.

Troy Aikman

Despite all the success, Aikman is generally still a pretty good guy and gracious signer—if you can get to him. In Dallas, the fans have no access to him unless you have a pass that gets you into the locker room. On visiting trips—finding and seeing him seems impossible.

I had a media pass for the Thanksgiving Day game against the Chiefs at Texas Stadium in 1995. I waited outside the Cowboys locker room after the game. Aikman was one of the last people out and signed for my friend and me, although he didn't seem too happy about it and did so without saying one word.

As a rookie, Aikman used to sign everything and even answer his mail. As he became more of a household name in the country, he just seemed to be unavailable. The last time I came into contact with Troy was at the Quarterback Challenge at Disney World in the spring of 1998. Troy was his usual polite self and signed when he could, although demand was incredible. He signed for me on both occasions I was near him, but kept walking and didn't stop. Once he reached his location he politely said, "Sorry, got to go," and left.

Basically, I have no complaints against Aikman, since he will still sign on most occasions if you can get near him. He has done a few paid appearances and private signings in the past few years, but the fees are steep: $75–$125. But for a guy who's taken a pounding from the hounds for the past decade, he still hangs in there for some freebies now and then.

So that's how the hounds see some of the better known athletes. Now it's on to what awaits us in the future in the collectible and autograph industries.

Chapter 10

The Future

The sports collectible and autograph industry will undergo many changes in the future. The "Internet Revolution" is leading the way, making autographs as accessible as your computer. Even athletes will refer autograph seekers to their websites rather than sign the items.

Sports coverage is greater now than any time in history. Turn on your television and you'll find sports events and coverage all day long. Cities now have competing sports radio stations. Television coverage of events like the X Games and the Olympics reach homes all over the world. More media creates more events and coverage, creating even more events and heroes. For a nation of couch potatoes, we can't get enough sports.

Eventually, look for more gossip and reporting on private lives to reach the sports market. We want to know more about our heroes. The public loves celebrity. Here's my thoughts on what you can expect in the future. . . .

Sports Collectibles

The market will get bigger as the computer creates easier access and a larger market. However, that market will stay flooded with products. There will be more people selling collectible items, and auctions will continue to record incredible prices for one-of-a-kind, rare items.

The public will be able to order directly from companies, third parties, individuals, and even the athletes themselves. The websites for many star athletes will be selling everything from game equipment to autographs. Many of the sales will be for private gain, while other athletes will donate sales to charitable causes.

Because there is no regulatory body, more forgeries and fakes will hit the marketplace. Quick hit-and-run profits will attract dishonest dealers. Consumers will continue to buy in good faith with little recourse or chance for refunds, many never finding justice. The sports collectible craze will eventually trickle down to the college level. Friends of star college athletes, seeing the opportunity to make fast money, will set up websites to sell those wares. Colleges and the National Collegiate Athletic Association (NCAA) will have a hard time stopping such practices. It can control athletes, but not private businesses—which is what these websites will be.

For the college athlete who has little spending money due to NCAA regulations—this will be a gold mine. They see the school making big money from their exploits, and won't feel badly about accepting money from other sources. Once the NCAA tries to rule against a few players selling their own property attorneys will become involved, creating an even bigger mess. It will mean more early departures to the pros rather than fighting the system. Thus far, the NCAA has been fortunate in the autograph craze, but the days are coming when it will have its hands full with this facet of sports collectibles.

Colleges will eventually be forced to change and allow their star players other sources of revenue, such as signings, appearances, and the direct sale of collectibles. There's too much money at stake. For a youngster with limited income throughout his life, the temptation may be too great to pass up such revenue sources. Schools will also have a difficult time policing such activities.

Who is hot in the collectibles market is ever changing. A player might be hot one season and fade the next. Free agency, injury, trades, criminal acts, shifting team fortunes, and sub-standard play can change exposure and demand. Poor performance may cool demand. Only a select few superstars will prevail.

The number of products today is unlimited. In most cases the supply will be greater than the demand, keeping values low. There's just too much being made today. If you are collecting today you are wise to do it for fun and enjoyment, with less emphasis on value. Enjoy the item. The financial return in most cases will be minimal.

Sports teams and major media will become partners in the marketplace. Marketing through the Internet and advertising will create more opportunities. A simple phone call and a credit card can get the item on its way, making it a quick process. The public will consider the teams and major media more reliable sources.

In the coming years, the public will have more places to buy more sports memorabilia and collectibles. You'll be able to place orders that can be answered on the same day. Never will obtaining your own personal sports memorabilia be so easy. So, if anybody can get the item on the Internet, what's the future of appearances?

Appearances

As long as there's money to be made, appearances by athletes will never die. The number of athletes making appearances, however, will decrease. Other factors provide reasons for fewer signing sessions.

As the older generation of athletes (1970 and before) passes on, there will be fewer athletes willing to replace them in the appearance pool. The older generation found appearances not only a great way to relive the past, but also supplement their incomes. It's less likely that the post-1970 athletes will be willing to hit the appearance circuit. They've experienced more of the autograph hysteria and probably have negative feelings toward the entire industry, as well as making much more income during their playing days. This means the necessity of such shows for financial gain is less likely.

Rising fees will discourage promoters. More private signings will be the rule. Appearances on sports shows selling sports collectibles will increase, especially for networks such as QVC and Home Shopping Network. The validity of these purchases will help in the marketplace.

Promoters will have to rely on mail order to generate the necessary number of autographs to make money. Promoters with strong mail order reputations will have a greater chance of covering fees. The theme show, such as 500 Home Run Club, 300 Game Winners, 2000 Yard Rushers, or 20,000 Point Scorers will continue to find a place in the market with greater chance of success. They may be large financial risks, but if properly promoted, will bring huge rewards.

Since many of today's superstar athletes won't need to do appearances, they will turn their attention to foundations and charitable causes through signings and offerings on websites. This will be further welcomed by the teams, who frown upon paid appearances since they don't present a positive public impression for either team or athlete. Nobody likes the idea of looking greedy.

Teams will begin to write agreements in contracts either assisting in fund-raising, or paying the athletes outright for not doing paid appearances while they are team members. The players themselves will have websites detailing their efforts and how the public can partake. The websites will offer a personalized photo for a specific donation to the foundation or charity. The bigger-name stars will have paid staff controlling the operation.

Teams entering into marketing agreements with athletes is another possibility. This is another currently untapped form of revenue for both the team and athlete. The Internet should make this a reality. Player contracts can allow appearances for them at team or charitable functions. What could be better than to have the athletes signing free at a team party honoring all top-level season ticket holders? It's an easy addendum to the player's contract.

Another factor is endorsement money. When an athlete today can make thousands and even millions of dollars for just using or wearing a certain shoe or piece of clothing, there is less need for extra income. In many cases, the companies may have clauses in player contracts prohibiting appearances for others, especially when a fee is attached to the autograph.

Hall of Famers and long-time superstars will always have a place in the autograph world. It is their fees and willingness to partake in signings that will determine who does appearances and who does not. It's all a matter of money and the direction from which the money is coming. If promoters, teams, and companies meet the athlete's price, there will continue to be appearances, private signings, and exclusive agreements.

Accessibility

Although the true hounds will always find a way to create autograph opportunities, it will be made more difficult by obstacles and restrictions. Getting near the players will be next to impossible.

Teams will have fenced-in parking areas, security guards in hotels to screen "loiterers," and the players themselves will just say "no" more often. Even in charitable outings, players will be able to fend off requests with references to their websites and other places selling such memorabilia. Also, there will be increased demands at such functions as more and more people take advantage of the chance to obtain signatures.

The lesser-known and common players will still be cooperative, but even their accessibility and cooperation will often hurt the chance of signing. Hounds will still prefer the stars, but won't often pass up others, which, after all, do have some monetary value. Once a player becomes more well known, he'll see the website route as the way to lighten his load. Even lesser names can tire of constant autograph requests.

Players linked with charitable causes and foundations will be able to say that signing via the Internet assures the charity, cause, or athlete of some direct benefit. Teams will endorse the idea of charitable websites and even have them as links with their internet addresses.

Exclusive contracts and agreements with teams, companies, or third parties could also play a factor in accessibility. The athletes can refer to such sites with their requests. Exclusives will be a gamble for the company, but smart agreements will have an enforcement clause that will penalize the athlete for signing under other circumstances, or bad behavior.

As previously stated, today's athletes will probably prefer to avoid public appearances, mainly because they won't need the money. Private signings will be preferred, since it's an easier process and there's no public or media to face. Those team contracts again may discourage or even prohibit appearances where a fee is to be charged for the autograph.

The signing habits of today's athletes will also affect the ability of anyone to obtain autographs. Although there's much lip service about "good public relations and signing autographs," there is no duty to do so. With or without face-to-face encounters, the athletes don't have to sign. Instead, they must come to the public—and this is happening less and less. In many cases the athletes are busy with pre-game preparation and don't want to be bothered. They are learning to refuse much more easily . . . and much sooner.

Those who do sign will certainly place limits, such as personalizations only, one each, specific items only, not in hotels, etc. In charitable outings, the mood will be more like "anything goes," but expect restrictions there, also. Rules will be established for the entire setting and then enforced. Security guards may help enforce those rules. Demand will eliminate second signatures.

Even signatures that are provided free could be different from paid ones. In paid outings, players may sign their complete names, while in free situations just one name and a number. Expect the freebies to have the worst penmanship—intentional or not.

Once upon a time, there were more people wanting to get into the promotional game who were willing to pay the fees of the athletes. With the continual rise in appearance fees, the shrinking dealer base, and the cost to promote such events, there's fewer willing to join. The promoter must feel sure it is a lock, yet realize the gamble. Most people won't take such a large risk. Charging over $20 for an autograph becomes a risky proposition. Remember that even a superstar like Ken Griffey, Jr. can be a tough sell because of a high autograph fee.

Lastly, consider the ever-increasing demand for autographs. More and more, the public is learning about the value of such items. There are more people joining the ranks of hounds everyday. At public functions, everyone, whether a collector or not, wants an autograph—most of which will be signed on items that will have no long-term value. However, more people are learning what is valuable to have signed and then trying to do so. It also leaves no doubt about the validity of the signature. There is no better assurance than getting the signature in person.

Place yourself in the position of Joe Superstar. Everywhere you go, you're treated like royalty and beseeched for autographs and photographs. Like anyone else, you'll have good days and bad days. The question is how you'll deal with it. Some enjoy it, others live with it, and still others come to despise it. Seeing many of the same people asking again and again sours many on signing altogether. Unfortunately, many of today's athletes are joining the ranks of non-signers.

Protecting Yourself

As the market expands with little regulation, there will be more opportunities for forgeries to enter the marketplace. So how does one interested in collecting autographs protect himself? Although there is no foolproof method, steps can be taken to decrease your chance of being taken.

As previously stated, getting the autographs in person is by far the best method of knowing the items are authentic. If it's a show appearance, insist on a ticket stub or notarized certificate on the spot. For a charitable event, get a copy of the program or have a photo taken when the item is being signed. Write down the date and place and keep it alongside the item. Although you may know it's real, the buyer wants to be confident, too.

Use the mail to order autographs from shows. Mailing to teams, residences, or third parties provides no guarantee you will get an actual signature. Do your homework before making a purchase. Study the signature, ask the experts, insist on a lifetime guarantee, and find out about the dealer and item before making a purchase. If you don't feel comfortable, don't buy it. Don't fall for the hype.

Price should not be the determining factor in buying memorabilia. Peace of mind for the buyer should top all other concerns. If possible, deal directly with the source through his own websites or other link. This is another reason why dealing directly with the signer will continue to gain momentum and eventually become the preferred method of purchase.

If you become a hound, prepare for frustration. You may sit in a hotel lobby for hours, only to find out your subject left through a side door. You may be refused. You may get a scribble instead of an autograph. You may have to be obnoxious to be noticed. At times, you'll consider it a complete waste of time.

However, many times you will get the chance to meet and even talk for short time with some of the greatest athletes in the world. You'll have a memory of those meetings for life. You'll build a collection of sports memorabilia that will impress others and constantly increase in value, something of a lifelong tangible asset.

Your time and efforts will produce keepsakes. You can also build a collection through purchasing the items, or attending autograph shows and appearances.

Being a hound is still unlikely for most collectors. Time is the major factor. Most memorabilia will still be handled through the marketplace. As the consumer, you'll have the ultimate say in who, what, and how to collect autographs and memorabilia. You'll help set the price, demand, and, in many cases, the availability.

Just be careful . . . it's a real jungle out there.

Chapter 11

The Conclusion:
What's It All Mean?

Since the beginning of the book you have read about the autograph industry and many of the athletes in it. You have learned much about each.

Sports collectibles, once a value was established for the first one, have become a part of American culture. Worshipping athletes and teams will always exist—and more than ever, we are willing to give second and third chances to our heroes. Sports as a whole receives much more credit for its importance to our daily lives and society than it deserves. But in most cases, sports only entertain us. They won't feed, clothe, or shelter us. Regardless, we love our teams and athletes.

Sports has its good and bad guys. It's how the athletes handle the adulation that gives us an impression of these celebrities. We expect more of our heroes and in many cases, they fail to measure up. Trouble also seems to grab the headlines. Too often, we'll overlook an athlete's negative qualities if he can help us win.

We don't know much about our heroes, other than what is spoon fed or choreographed by the media and its spin doctors. By obtaining an autograph, we feel as though we have a piece of the athlete for our enjoyment. Adding to its attraction is its monetary value. Their photographs look good on our walls and provide us with the feeling we've got a piece of them with us.

In the privacy of autograph settings, you can learn much about the personalities of our heroes. Athletes can come off as good guys or jerks, and in a 30-minute period can exhibit behavior of both. If you want to find out what your sports hero is really like, put him in a crowded room with 100 people clamoring for a free autograph.

As far as paying for the signature, as long as there's a willing buyer for an autograph, there will be people trying to get it and sell it. If enough are willing to pay the price, there will be appearances for pay when athletes are paid with fees charged by promoters and passed on to the public.

The capitalist system is at work in the autograph industry, including scam artists willing to knowingly sell you a forgery. Price, supply, and demand are all factors that figure into the equation.

In 1996, *The Washington Post* ran a story reporting the estimated value of the sports collectible industry as $750 million annually. An Upper Deck® official estimated the total annual transactions at $500 million. Either figure indicates the immense interest and money in the sports collectible and autograph industries.

Could all this be a case of misplaced hero worship? We love those who can throw touchdown passes, hit home runs, stuff the ball through the hoop, or score goals and play in the best leagues in the world in their respective sports. When you consider that only about 1,500 can play in the NFL, 300 in the NBA, 700 in Major League Baseball and 600 in the NHL each year, this is indeed elite company. Of those, only about 20 percent will achieve star status. It is rarified air. Therefore, the pay scale for their skills reflects their ability to reach that top level. Sure, it's more than we pay our teachers, day care workers, and others entrusted with the daily care and decision-making that affects our lives in many more important ways. It's no wonder many of these athletes develop inflated egos and a defiant attitude. They've been told all their lives how great they are.

My father, who died in 1997, will always be my hero. I've never seen highlights of my dad on any sports shows. He never dunked a basketball, hit a major league home run, or scored an NFL touchdown. But he did assume the role of husband and father for his four children and quietly went about his daily life of feeding, clothing, and sheltering his family. More importantly, he taught his children honest, positive values and did so with a loving hand. He was always there when we needed him. I don't know much about the personal lives of many of the athletes I have hosted through the years, but I did know the daily struggles of my parents 365 days a year—not only on game days.

My father had only an eighth grade education. He had to quit school to help support his family and help raise his brothers and sisters. Later in life, after 25 years of hard labor in a mill, he started a coin collecting business that eventually earned him enough funds to live comfortably, reaching over $1 million in sales annually at one point. More importantly, he enjoyed himself as the head of his own business, the real American Dream.

More amazing is that as a society we seem more fascinated with the anti-hero role model types such as Dennis Rodman, O.J. Simpson, Latrell Sprewell, and Dennis Scott.

Scott made headlines in 1998 when he exploded at a children's fantasy camp in Sterling, Virginia. Scott had threatened retirement if the Orlando Magic didn't meet his salary demands, and then brought it all to head at the camp. With obscenity-laced rap music playing in the background, Scott told the kids, "Don't ask me for autographs, ask me about the rage that exists inside me." At the time, he had one year remaining on his $3 million contract. Most of John Q. Public would have gladly traded places with him.

In my opinion, he should have been banned from the league permanently; instead, he just found another team and still plays today. This shuffling of malcontents and lawbreakers seem to happen with more frequency each year. Leagues can talk about role models and what's good for the fans, but "their actions speak louder than their words," one of my dad's favorite sayings.

The purpose of this book wasn't to berate you for your choice of role models. In this country you have the freedom to believe as you want, thanks to some real heroes who shed their blood and gave their lives for that right.

The vast majority of today's professional athletes are genuine people of good character. Most realize the gift they've been given, and return the favor with assistance to hundreds of charitable causes. They, too, go about raising families and conducting their daily business. They, too, have kids in Little League and school plays. Only their lives become more public. Our images are too often formed solely from their exploits on the playing field.

God blessed me with 15 years of rubbing shoulders with many of the greatest athletes of all time. Andy Warhol was right—I did have my 15 minutes of fame. What's more, I enjoyed every minute of it, even the unpleasant ones. It has provided me with a lifetime of memories and mementos.

I hoped you've enjoyed reading all about those times. The pleasure's been all mine. Stay healthy, live right, and God bless.

See ya next book.

THE END

Index

BE A PART OF SIGN THIS II

I'm looking for your autograph experiences, especially humorous, offbeat or unusual happenings. Your stories could be a part of *Sign This II*, the follow-up to this book. Surely you have one or two tales you'd like to share with others.

Mail or e-mail your entries to me [bunevich@earthlink. net]. Entries must be typewritten, signed, and include a return address and phone number. We'll contact those chosen for this next great literary work. You can send entries to me:

Tom Bunevich
6805 Grand Bahama Dr.,
Tampa, FL 33615

No phone calls, please.

The deadline is March 1, 2001. At that time we'll contact those selected. You don't have to be a great writer; just tell the story. Our editors will improve your story, then you, too, can see your name in publication.

Finally, there will be no compensation for your contributions. Consider it your gift to the sports collectibles or autograph industry. Please send true stories only. We want the truth, not your imagination.

We'll be waiting for your stories.